The Human Resource Professional's Guide to Change Management

The Human Resource Professional's Guide to Change Management

Practical Tools and Techniques to Enact Meaningful and Lasting Organizational Change

Melanie J. Peacock, PhD, MBA, CPHR

 BUSINESS EXPERT PRESS

The Human Resource Professional's Guide to Change Management: Practical Tools and Techniques to Enact Meaningful and Lasting Organizational Change

First published in 2017 by
Business Expert Press, LLC
222 East 46th Street, New York, NY 10017
www.businessexpertpress.com

ISBN-13: 978-1-63157-766-6 (paperback)
ISBN-13: 978-1-63157-767-3 (e-book)

Business Expert Press Human Resource Management and Organizational Behavior Collection

Collection ISSN: 1946-5637 (print)
Collection ISSN: 1946-5645 (electronic)

Cover and interior design by Exeter Premedia Services Private Ltd., Chennai, India

First edition: 2017

10 9 8 7 6 5 4 3 2 1

Printed in the United States of America.

To Dr. Julie Chen
Throughout, and no matter what life's changes,
forever my friend

Abstract

The ability to help an organization effectively deal with change is a key competency that all Human Resource (HR) professionals must possess. However, many people in the HR function have not received any formal training or instruction on how to fulfill this key role. Further, HR professionals are often paralyzed or frustrated by employees' and senior management attitudes and practices, thereby feeling left out of the change process entirely or powerless within it.

This book provides HR professionals with key concepts and practical techniques to successfully launch, support, and sustain change management initiatives within their organizations. Pragmatic tools and explanations will illuminate critical change management competencies and processes, thereby enabling HR professionals to take on strategic and active roles as they guide and lead stakeholders to successfully deal with change. Further, understanding of one's own reactions to change and how to harness this energy will also be explored to further assist HR professionals to effectively manage and guide change. Key questions posed at the end of each chapter allow for personal reflection and growth, further providing for development of skills relating to change management.

This text is an excellent resource for HR students, those new to practicing HR and seasoned HR professionals alike.

Keywords

change, change management, human resource management, human resource professionals, organizational change, transform, transition

Contents

Preface xi

Acknowledgments xiii

Chapter 1   Why Change Management Matters to
             Human Resource Professionals 1

Chapter 2   Forces for Change 9

Chapter 3   Categories of Organizational Change 19

Chapter 4   A Formula for Managing Change 31

Chapter 5   Resistance to Change 45

Chapter 6   Launching Change 59

Chapter 7   Maintaining Change Momentum 73

Chapter 8   Communication 81

Chapter 9   Bringing It All Together: The HR Professional's Role 93

Notes 103

References 107

Index 111

Preface

Enter the words "books on change management" into a search engine and a multitude of titles will appear. So why the need for *this* text? The numerous items available address an important topic, but typically from the viewpoint of stakeholders (such as employees) experiencing organizational change or people in management positions who must lead change. Human Resource (HR) professionals have a critical role to play during times of change, but must utilize unique skills and processes in order to do so. As such, the way in which employees, leaders, and other stakeholders deal with, and respond to change, is not the same way that HR professionals can and should. HR professionals are tasked with bringing organizational change to life, and sustaining the amendments, often without the formal authority to do so. Further, I've regularly heard from students and clients that while HR people play a critical part within managing change, this occurs without formal training and exposure to change theory and HR-specific change competencies.

Therefore, this book provides a needed resource as it is written specifically from an HR point of view. This text addresses distinct skills and processes needed to enact meaningful and lasting organizational change from the perspective of HR professionals and explores key topics, theories, and the practical application of these elements. As well, through questions posed at the conclusion of each chapter, readers can apply the material presented to the HR roles in their own organizations and their personal situations as well.

This book therefore specifically enhances change management capabilities for HR professionals. Further, it is my deep hope that the journey through this material will provide the reader with career and life-altering skills and competencies and therefore leave one changed, for the better, both professionally and personally.

Acknowledgments

This book could not have been written without help and support from many people, including the wonderful team at Business Expert Press. Specific gratitude to Rod Banister and Rob Zwettler for endorsing the concept for this text and encouraging me to write it.

A special thank you to Dr. Alex Lefter and Cameron Simpson for reading and reviewing the draft version and for your comments and feedback, which served to enhance the final product.

Many of the ideas and insights shared throughout the text have been drawn from my interactions and conversations with students and clients. These peoples' desire to grow and make organizations, and therefore ultimately the lives of others better, are commendable and motivate me to want to do the same.

Alia Azim-Garcia, Landis Jackson, and Janice MacPherson also need to be recognized. Your constant pursuit of excellence and courage to continuously embrace change is inspirational. Further, your backing and words of reinforcement helped to sustain my momentum throughout the creation of this book.

I also thank Steve Browne, who I have never met in-person, but who is an HR friend and colleague through various social media platforms. Talk about an example of change! Through these resources, which years ago I would not have envisioned using, I have been able to learn from a true champion of people and HR. Thanks Steve, for constantly pushing the HR community to grow and develop.

Last, but certainly not least, I thank my amazing family: Cam, Miranda, Joely, Eric, and Dash. While change is constant, my love for you will forever remain.

CHAPTER 1

Why Change Management Matters to Human Resource Professionals

Be the change that you wish to see in the world.

—Mahatma Gandhi

The skills and competencies needed to succeed as a Human Resource (HR) professional are complex and involve a dynamic interaction of many differing and diverse capabilities. As the HR profession has grown and evolved, so too have the required qualities and abilities of HR practitioners. No longer seen as a dumping ground for employees with performance issues that cannot be corrected, or a holding spot for someone filling time until retirement, the HR department is now valued as a critical resource in helping organizations achieve their strategic outcomes.[1] As such, a key reason that change management matters to HR professionals is due to the changes and evolution of the profession itself.[2] In order to stay abreast of the demands and rigor within the profession, HR professionals must be capable of adapting and responding to change, thereby altering their own competencies and knowledge. Further, when examining the qualifications within various HR designations (e.g., CPHR, CHRP, CHRL, SHRM-CP),[3] the ability to effectively deal with and facilitate organizational change is highlighted. The expectation that HR professionals are well versed in the complexities of change management, and how to help organizations effectively utilize, benefit from, and sustain change, is clearly detailed within these designations.

As well, it is readily acknowledged that a company will only succeed if it has the correct people, in the correct places, doing the correct things at the correct times.[4] As such, HR professionals are tasked with playing a key part in ensuring that this strategic alignment and configuration occurs. So what does this really mean? How do HR professionals ensure that a company succeeds and achieves desired strategic outcomes? Are HR professionals really *people-people*, and is liking and understanding others enough to bring about key organizational results? The balance between focusing on operational requirements and attending to peoples' needs and wants is an issue that HR professionals should readily acknowledge and must not shy away from. As such, it is imperative that HR professionals be ever aware of the changes that organizations experience, and how to assist with these amendments through the dynamic interplay of meeting both the organization's (operational) and peoples' (emotive) needs. This again highlights the need for change management competencies.

Is It *Human* Resources or *Humane* Resources?

When I first meet people they usually ask me about my work. When I explain that I am an HR professional, the next part of the conversation is inevitably predictable. I cringe when people tell me that since I'm in HR I must like people and respond by saying "Oh, indeed I like people. I like to fire people, I like to tell people they did not get the job, I like to tell them that they are not meeting performance expectations...." This typically puts a quick end to the dialogue, but the serious and truthful nature of my reply should not be easily dismissed. The practice of HR often involves tough decisions and actions—from terminations to disciplinary meetings to assisting employees during times of grief and illness. This type of work certainly speaks to having a skill set that encompasses much more than just liking people, thus clearly demonstrating a change from previous labels of *personnel*, or the people who must enjoy dealing with employees.

HR professionals are tasked with ensuring that organizations achieve their objectives with and through the most valuable assets—their people.[5] This is not easy or simple work and means having to, at times, engage in difficult conversations and issues. It can, at times, also involve celebrating and recognizing good work and accomplishments. Through a strategic lens, HR professionals are viewed as those who understand how to plan for and implement policies and procedures that enable employees and organizations to succeed. In summary, being an HR professional means having to deal with an organization's human assets in good times and bad, from the start of someone's employment to the end of their tenure with a company, and through the myriad of situations that arise in between. The altering and varying circumstances that HR professionals become involved in further speak to the importance of change management, as this role is not static with a limited set of requirements. As such, HR professionals who understand and appropriately use change management tools and techniques are better able to do their jobs, as the nature of the work requires someone who is able to quickly adjust and meet new or altering demands.

The Heart of the Matter

Dealing with *people issues* means dealing with people. At first glance this appears rather simplistic or repetitive, but it is important to remember that *human* beings are the central component to the HR profession. The ability to deal with people in a strategic, competent, and yet compassionate manner is critical to the enactment of an HR professional's role. As such, it is not unreasonable to expect HR people to be able to communicate with, engage with, and work with others, with a goal of achieving strategic outcomes.[6] Therefore, HR professionals are often seen as the *heart* of an organization.

For this analogy to hold true it is important to remember that the heart is only one critical, yet admittedly very important, component of how the whole body works. The heart helps keep other processes and functions within the body (the organization) aligned and working well to ensure the desired overall result, which is a healthy and high-functioning entity. When the heart stops or does not work as it should, no other functions within the body will fare well. As such, concrete (often difficult) and strategic decisions and actions pertaining to diet, exercise, and lifestyle choices have to be made to ensure that the heart functions properly, thereby ensuring an effective and top performing body. This is similar to the tactical decisions that HR must develop and implement so that an organization operates effectively and produces top results. While very practical in its operation, the human heart is also known for having the capacity for emotion and dealing with issues in more than just a rational manner. So, defining HR as the heart of an organization is again rather appropriate. An organization's operational functions must be attended to and adhered to, often resulting in strategic conversations, decisions, and actions.[7] However, emotive components must be nurtured and honored as well. As such, the practice of HR is not a choice between two areas of focus, but rather a way of finding pathways to ensure effective operations and functionality while honoring and upholding the emotive elements within an organization. While simple and basic, at the heart of the matter (pun intended), the truth is that accomplishing great results through both function and form (operational and emotional effectiveness) is not a simple task. Engaging and motivating people, while representing the interests of both employers and employees, is a delicate, multifaceted juggling act, and ever evolving challenge. As such, HR professionals must be adept at managing change as the interests of employers and employees are dynamic and require an ability to keep up with the changing, often conflicting requirements, as they present themselves. This leads to a further complexity for an HR professional and presents a potential challenge within this role, as both employers and employees are viewed as clients.

Who's the Boss?

A difficult question that HR professionals must resolve is who they actually work for and represent. Is it the employers or is it the employees? I argue that this is not an either or query, but that through careful, well-thought-out, and skillful plans and actions, both groups' needs are addressed. In fact, it is only through meeting the needs of both groups that organizations will truly succeed. However, this is not an easy outcome to achieve. Often the needs and requirements of employers are seen to be in conflict with those of employees.[8] This is not just the case in unionized environments, although these more regimented workplaces often seem to amplify these divergent interests. In unionized and nonunionized work settings alike, employers' desired outcomes, and the pathways to achieving them, often do not align with employees' needs and interests. For example, an organization may want to serve clients across a diverse geographic area, but employees may dislike travel and time away from home. Such requirements could be seen as distracting from employees achieving a work–life balance. As another example, a company may want employees to put in extra hours in order produce a certain amount of products and employees may have health and safety concerns around this due to resulting fatigue. Situations abound where employers' and employees' needs, motivators, and desired outcomes do not align. As such, it is imperative that an HR practitioner be able to find the common and overlapping requirements for management and employees and in doing so *change* employers' and employees' perspectives and understanding in order to create synergies within and across the company. This, in turn, reduces barriers and perceived distances between people while providing opportunities to achieve sought-after results. This need to find commonality and overlap exists across many of the practices and processes most commonly dealt with under the HR umbrella such as the following: Recruitment and Selection, Orientation, Work Design, Compensation, Learning and Development, and Performance Management. For example, how can the need for new employees to be socialized and welcomed to an organization be balanced with an employer's desire to get people working as soon as possible? Or, how can an employee's need for a fair and sufficient salary be met while still ensuring that a company remains profitable? So while discussions continue about how HR professionals can find a *seat at the decision-making table* and how HR professionals can *truly be viewed as strategic partners,* the reality is quite simple—find ways to change employers' and employees' limited and self-serving views and find ways to develop and implement strategic processes, practices, and policies that meet the needs of both parties in meaningful and practical ways, thereby ensuring focused efforts on achieving desired company objectives. In order to accomplish this, HR professionals must have a solid understanding of change management principles as organizations continue to evolve and grow. In other words, HR professionals must develop, implement, and monitor processes, practices, and policies that meet the needs of both employers and employees within an environment that is ever fluctuating. In doing so, HR professionals must also be seen as those who can guide and facilitate others on how to effectively use and follow new processes, practices, and policies. These expected competencies clearly necessitate that HR professionals are well versed in change management tools and techniques.

Summary

Evolving requirements within the profession itself necessitate that HR professionals be able to skillfully change and enhance their own capabilities in order to remain current and relevant in the field. HR professionals who cannot manage change will not be able to evolve and develop themselves in response to the advancing requirements within this specialized discipline. Further, HR professionals balance operational and emotive needs within an organization and the facets within these requirements are ever shifting. Therefore skillful change management assists HR professionals to meet the fluctuating needs of both employers and employees, thereby ensuring desired organizational outcomes can be achieved.

It is clear that HR professionals need to possess change management capabilities. However, knowing *what* needs to change (i.e., processes, practices, and policies) is not enough. In addition to this, it is critical that HR professionals have a deep and rich understanding of the complexities around *why* change should occur and *how* to enact effective and lasting change. While HR professionals are typically the people whom others turn to for guidance and advice on what responses are required to deal with change, HR professionals are also expected to provide advice and guidance on *how* to effectively manage change. This point is critical and bears repeating: Knowing *what* needs to change is not sufficient, as HR professionals must also be skilled in recognizing *why* change is necessary and *how* to manage change. The remainder of this book will help you do all of this. Chapter 2 reviews the driving forces for change and explores why change may be required at various times in an organization's evolution. Chapter 3 then reviews the different categories of change organizations typically face and why it is important to differentiate among varying types of modifications. Chapter 4 addresses a formula for managing change, while Chapter 5 focuses on resistance, which is one specific element within the formula. Chapters 6 and 7 then review specific tools and techniques to launch and sustain organizational change. This is followed in Chapter 8 by an exploration of important communication tools and techniques to use during times of change and Chapter 9 brings all ideas presented throughout the book together, highlighting the role that

HR professionals should play within change management, including the importance of self-exploration and self-development.

As such, your journey through this text will leave you with a deeper understanding of how to, in your role as an HR professional, help organizations enact meaningful and lasting change.

End of Chapter Questions

- Based on your own experiences, what advice would you give to someone having to deal with conflicting interests and needs from employers and employees?
- What has been the biggest change you have noted in the HR profession over the past five years and how has this impacted and influenced you as an HR practitioner?
- What do you anticipate will be the one or two biggest changes that will occur within the HR profession within the next five years? How are you preparing yourself for this?
- What are three key points of learning that you want to take away from reading this text?

CHAPTER 2

Forces for Change

No matter what people tell you, words and ideas can change the world.
—Robin Williams

A key part of managing change is understanding *why* change is required, or in other words being clear about the driving force behind a change. Many elements that drive organizational change will impact and influence processes, practices, and policies that an HR professional is responsible for developing or implementing, and therefore ultimately changing. When an HR professional has a deep and rich understanding of *why* change is needed (i.e., what is driving a change) appropriate actions can be implemented. In other words, knowing *why* change is required allows for the appropriate decision of *what* to change as a consequence of this driving force. Further, knowing why change is necessary may allow for a change to occur in advance as an anticipatory measure. This is of critical importance. An HR professional who is aware of forces for change is often able to be proactive and make amendments before difficulties arise.[1] Enacting changes that avoid legal, operational, and strategic difficulties is a key way in which HR professionals are able to provide value within their roles.

Preemptive responses to forces for change are not always possible and as such, appropriate reactions are also something that an HR professional must be capable of. Being able to quickly and effectively adjust organizational processes, practices, and policies in response to changing requirements is also an expectation of HR professionals and therefore a clear picture of the change driver is once again required.

In order to understand why a change is required, and then appropriately deal with this either proactively or as a responsive action, HR professionals must continuously monitor and stay abreast of key elements or factors that impact their work. These factors, which are common drivers of change, can be explored as the HR professional's landscape.[2]

The HR Professional's Landscape

Developing and implementing significant and pragmatic organizational processes, practices, and policies that meet employer and employee requirements with the end goal of achieving an organization's strategic goals necessitates that HR professionals understand:

- Legislative requirements
- Industry trends
- Labor market conditions
- Competitors
- Customer demands
- Organizational strategies

While this list is not exhaustive, it certainly points to and addresses key factors that HR professionals must continuously review and address.[3] Further, these areas that HR professionals must be aware of are not static and changes within each of these elements are what typically initiate or necessitate changes within an organization. Legislative, industry, and labor market considerations are typically grouped together as environmental drivers of change. Competitors and customer demands capture market forces for change and organizational strategies align with internally driven initiatives that serve as an impetus for change.[4] As Figure 2.1 illustrates, all forces for change interact and influence one other with further complexities arising as each of the previously noted elements continuously evolves and shifts.

An HR professional must be able to stay abreast of new requirements and developments within each of these key areas and the changes that are

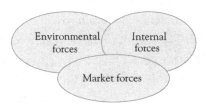

Figure 2.1 Forces for change

necessitated by these amendments. As well, HR professionals must also continue to be aware of how and if multiple drivers of change are in play and how they are impacting each other. As such, exploration of each area within an HR professional's landscape, and how it is a driving force for change (i.e., *why* change is needed) along with examples of preemptive or reactionary responses (i.e., *what* needs to change) is warranted.

Legislative Requirements

At all times, legislative compliance must be at the front of mind for HR professionals.[5] Employment standards, occupational health and safety standards, and human rights are some examples of areas covered under specific legal requirements.[6] As the world and its value and belief systems change, so too does the law. An example of this falls under the duty to accommodate employees due to protected grounds. For example, as per current legislation in Canada, family status is now viewed as something that employers must consider and provide reasonable accommodation for when requested to do so.[7] This has led to changes in the way in which shift work is scheduled and the amount of notice that needs to be provided when employees are required on site. Another example of value systems influencing legal issues can be seen through the removal of mandatory retirement (exceptions apply due to safety-sensitive roles) as this is seen as age discrimination.[8] As such, an organization's policies and processes had to be changed at one point to ensure that employees were not being forced out, and that incorrect assumptions regarding future staffing levels or predictions for recruitment were not being made based upon forced employee departures, which would be deemed illegal. Therefore, the ability to monitor amendments to legal requirements and ensure ongoing compliance by an organization through alteration of key processes and guidelines, both proactively and reactively, is certainly a key change competency that an HR professional must possess.

Industry Trends

HR professionals must have a thorough understanding of the industry that an organization operates in and the critical indicators of trends within this context.[9] Industry trends alert an HR professional to upcoming organizational changes that are required in order for a company to remain competitive. Illustrations of this are prevalent in heavily resource-based industries such as oil and gas. As an example, decreasing commodity prices signal that cost-cutting measures will need to be addressed and these most often impact HR-related areas such as recruitment, staffing levels, and training and development budgets. HR professionals must keep abreast of key indicators (e.g., trending and anticipated fluctuations to commodity prices) that signal upcoming changes within an industry. By doing so, changes can be anticipated in advance. These leading indicators result in well planned and thought-out strategies that negate drastic reactions to unforeseen circumstances. For example, knowing that the industry will be facing a decreased demand for workers, staffing levels can be addressed through normal attrition or a hiring freeze, thereby minimizing the number of employees who have to be terminated when commodity prices, and resulting profits, decrease.

As another example, the grocery industry has changed to allow for online ordering and product collection from the parking lot.[10] As this type of shopping option becomes a standard procedure, and more of a normalized option within this industry, organizations will have to ensure that they have changed what skills they seek in employees (employees will need computer literacy to read and understand orders), will have to alter training programs to ensure that employees know how to perform these new functions and may likely have to alter methods of evaluating customer service skills, due to the different ways in which employees and customers will interact. In summary, the HR professional who is knowledgeable about industry changes is able to anticipate, plan for, and/or implement organizational consequences of these industry alterations and thereby demonstrate change management competencies.

Labor Market Conditions

Just as focus on industry is important, so too is understanding labor market trends. Availability of workers, especially those with unique or specialized skills, is critical to the ongoing success of an organization.[11] Therefore, an HR professional must always be aware of alterations to the supply of workers resulting from issues such as demographic changes, mobility of the workforce and shifting educational levels. As an example, workers who have retired from their full-time positions but still seek employment have resulted in a different pool of potential employees whom organizations can attract to fill part-time roles. This, in turn, requires an alteration to recruitment and selection strategies in order to better align with this different target group of candidates. As another example, awareness that people with key education and skills live in certain geographic areas allows for planning and implementation of recruitment initiatives aimed at these key resources. Once again, knowledge regarding the characteristics of potential workers in the labor market allows an HR professional to amend recruitment and selection practices, thereby altering processes to attract key human resources and filling positions in a strategic manner that responds to the composition of the workforce. The ability to alter recruitment and selection practices and procedures, in anticipation of or in response to this environmental driver of change, is just one example of how an HR professional utilizes change management capabilities to enhance strategic outcomes.

Competitors

It is critical for HR professionals to know which organizations should be considered as competitors. A simple way to determine competitive forces involves listing organizations, either currently in operation or potentially starting operations, that offer products or services that would replace or substitute those offered by a company.[12] Once known, activities of the competition must consistently be monitored and appropriate responses often necessitate a change in an organization's policies and processes to meet, or exceed, offerings from competitive entities. As an example, when a competitor begins to publicize a program where employees are given time off to volunteer in the community, a company may choose to respond in kind. Implementation of their own employee volunteer program may be carried out in order to maintain a strong presence of social responsibility in the community, thereby keeping customers who value this, as well as to continue attracting new employees and retaining the current workforce who believe in this type of program and employee benefit. This would then necessitate the development and implementation of key HR policies and procedures around an employee volunteer program, thereby producing change in the benefits offered to the workforce.

As another example, a competitor may alter/increase their hours of operation and in order to keep current clients by matching services, an organization may have to follow suit thereby revising employees' working hours and shifts. Again, this would involve changes to key HR policies and procedures such as scheduling and compensation. The preceding examples highlight how competitors can influence actions that organizations have to take and as such, how actions from opponents are a force for change. Therefore, an HR professional will be expected to provide advice and guidance on how to change critical processes, practices, and policies in order to keep an organization viable against the actions of competitor organizations, once again highlighting the importance of change management competencies in this role.

Customer Demands

Being agile and responsive to shifting customer requirements is critical to ensure an organization's ongoing success. As such, an HR professional must be able to amend key policies and practices in order to ensure that these demands are met. As an example, when consumers demand healthier menu choices, employees need to receive training on how to prepare, promote, and serve these new food selections. Or, when a shifting customer base requires that a company's services be offered in different languages, employees must be trained to acquire this new skill or new employees, who meet this requirement, will need to be hired. The preceding examples are merely two descriptions of how an HR professional will have to adapt and revise current processes, practices, and policies in order to effectively respond to shifting customer needs, thereby ensuring the retention of clients. Numerous other examples of customer-driven needs are continuously evolving and presenting requirements for change within organizations, which in turn necessitate alterations to company policies, processes, and procedures. As such, the ability to effectively develop and implement changes, again proactively or in response to changes, is once again seen as critical within the HR professional's landscape.

Organizational Strategies

There are numerous strategic decisions that a company may make pertaining to its internal operations.[13] For example, a company may decide on using a team-based approach to completing work, or may determine that it wants employees to display a more creative and less risk adverse approach to their work. Each of these potential scenarios would necessitate that an HR professional implement changes to complement these company directives. For example, when a team-based approach to work is implemented, the way employees receive feedback and coaching will need to be altered, thereby necessitating that a new performance management system be developed and implemented. Processes focused on individual behaviors and outcomes would no longer align with the organizational desire for team focus and a change in monitoring and evaluating performance would need to ensue. Further, compensation policies and processes would also have to be amended to complement and reinforce a focus on team outcomes in lieu of individual achievements. Changes to compensation would also have to be implemented should an organizational directive to encourage creativity and risk-taking be implemented. In this particular example, an HR professional needs to have a strong understanding of what changes are necessary in order to align financial rewards with desired employee behavior, or people will not move away from safe, tried, and true actions that they know will result in receipt of monetary rewards. As the preceding examples highlight, as a driving force for change, organizational strategies demand that an HR professional possess strong change management abilities in order to amend other key organizational processes to align with and support the new company directives.

Summary

An organization is typically required to change in anticipation of, or in response to, key elements which are known as forces for change. These considerations typically impact organizational processes, practices, and policies that an HR professional is responsible for and therefore attention to these elements and the ability to be aware of *why* change is needed *and* *what* needs to be amended to allow for this change is critical. Given the elements within an HR professional's landscape are ever evolving, it is critical that an HR professional keep on top of these factors and amendments within them, thereby ensuring implementation of organizational change(s) to accommodate for, and capitalize on, these shifting environmental, market, and internally driven forces.

With a solid understanding of *why* change is needed and *what* needs to change, an HR professional must then be able to determine *how* best to implement and sustain required changes. The starting point for this is a clear understanding of what type of change is being addressed and this will be dealt with in Chapter 3.

End of Chapter Questions

- What is the primary force for change in your organization? What elements within this driving force have you had to respond to and what processes, practices, and policies have you changed in response to these?
- Given the elements with an HR professional's landscape, what do you anticipate as upcoming driving forces for change in your organization and how will you plan to respond?
- What element within an HR professional's landscape is often forgotten or given the least attention? Why do you think this occurs?
- What is a recent situation where a company failed to attend to a key element within an HR professional's landscape that changed and then subsequently faced poor outcomes or results? What is your key learning from this?
- In lieu of being labeled as a specific driving force for change, technology can be seen as embedded within various types of change, or as a catalyst for various forces for change. The online grocery shopping example provided in this chapter addresses altering use of technology as part of industry trends that are driving change. As another example, requirements for online apps and online access to company information could be viewed as a technological catalyst within customer demands as a force for change. Within which force for change

do you anticipate technology will have the most impact in your organization? What changes in policies, processes, and practices will you have to enact to help your organization prepare for, or react to, this?

CHAPTER 3

Categories of Organizational Change

If we don't change, we don't grow. If we don't grow, we aren't really living.

—Gail Sheehy

Change is here to stay. Change is ongoing. Change is required in order to survive and those who do not embrace and effectively deal with it are destined for failure. The clichés and quotes pertaining to change are familiar and the messaging continues to reinforce that change is not something that can be ignored or undervalued. Yet, there is lack of understanding about what change truly encompasses and involves or what change truly means.[1] A key part of this problem is that one singular word, *change*, is used to describe many diverse, complex, and multipurpose situations. People tend to singularly speak about change when they are actually describing vastly distinct scenarios that involve differing levels of resource commitment.[2] Just think about it. "I am going to change my socks" versus "I am going to change the world." Regardless of how fantastic a person's socks are, I am certain you will agree that the type of change envisioned in each of the previous statements is drastically different. Knowing *how* to effectively manage change therefore necessitates a solid understanding of the parameters of the change being addressed, or in other words what *type of change* is being dealt with. Without a thorough consideration of the type of change being addressed the sought-after results and benefits from the change may only be partially realized or may not be accomplished at all.

As well, knowing the type of change that is being addressed provides HR professionals with knowledge about the typical pitfalls that are encountered during these kinds of modifications. This, in turn, enables HR professionals to be better equipped to enact strategic change management competencies by anticipating, and therefore dealing with, things that can usually take a specific type of change initiative off track.

There are three categories of organizational changes that can occur: Tangential, Transitional and Transformational.[3]

Tangential Change

Many of the changes that people encounter in their everyday lives, both personally and professionally, are incremental or tangential. These are changes that happen very slowly and as such, often go unnoticed or unappreciated. As Figure 3.1 shows, tangential changes occur a little bit at a time over a lengthy period. As such, it is often difficult to recognize these individual gradual changes that ultimately, when taken into account as a sum of numerous small changes, can lead to vastly different circumstances. When my children were young and my family would see friends after some time apart, I would inevitably hear about how much the kids had grown. This made sense to me, as logically I knew they were changing, but because I saw them every day it was not until someone made note of these changes and overtly mentioned this to me that I was reminded of, and thus explicitly aware of, the changes that were occurring. It is rather like not seeing the forest for the trees or in this scenario, not seeing how

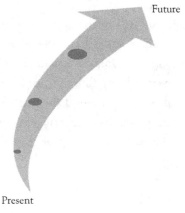

Present

Figure 3.1 Tangential change

the trees have developed until someone with a fresh perspective visits the forest after some time away from it. Gradual, or tangential change, is not readily obvious to those who live with or within it.

Organizations continuously go through these tangential changes and as such, one of the key change management competencies of an HR professional is to be aware of, acknowledge, and support these types of amendments.[4] Owing to the small and gradual nature of the changes, employees typically find their own unique, preferred, and simple ways to incorporate changes into their work and this leads to a lack of consistency in the way tasks are accomplished and work is completed. Or worse, employees may find ways to avoid the changes and forget about them altogether. This is one of the key issues with tangential changes—they can be ignored. HR professionals with strong change management competencies are therefore skilled at recognizing tangential changes and finding ways to ensure that they are effectively incorporated into employees' work and ultimately used to enhance an organization's strategic outcomes. Chapter 4 will address ways that HR professionals can ensure that this occurs, but before any action can be taken, the first step is to recognize that this type of tangential modification is occurring. As such, it is worthwhile to review examples of this category of change.

Examples of Tangential Change

As previously noted, tangential changes are the most common type of modifications that organizations experience. Another way to explain this is that employees have to *tweak* their work processes in order to accommodate a new requirement(s). Think about the following list and whether your company has encountered these or similar scenarios:

- A new product or service is introduced to add to (or slightly alter) current offerings.
- A new application is used to enhance current software.
- A new step is added to a production process.
- A step is taken out of a production process.
- A new form must be completed as part of a required reporting process.

Regardless of the specific tangential change, it is important to remember that when all of the little changes are taken into account in their entirety throughout the whole organization, these amendments actually have the potential for lasting and substantial consequences regarding the achievement of corporate outcomes. Tangential changes typically require an employee to change a process or work habit without altering mindset (i.e., focus on what is being done without elaborate or deep thinking about why the work needs to be done in this manner), but are nonetheless an important and critical part of the change landscape within organizations. Ignoring or avoiding these minor amendments diminishes organizational opportunities, outcomes, and potential for success.

Transitional Change

Transitional change is more complex than tangential change, as it involves replacing what is with something completely different. In lieu of slight amendments, transitional change involves creating an entirely new process or system. These types of amendments require employees to change their behaviors in order to complete new work and therefore necessitate new understanding of processes and requirements. In other words, as entire components of their work change, or in some cases entire roles need to change, employees must alter both behavior and mindset. A quick fix or quick amendment will not suffice, as in tangential change, and therefore more thought is required in order to enact the required modification. Transitional change is often thought of as a way to enhance processes, policies, or practices; how to replace an old way of doing things with the goal to create a new way of operating that is more efficient and effective.[5] As Figure 3.2 illustrates, transitional change involves moving from an old state to a new state over a set period of time using planned and deliberate actions to guide this process.

Given the intentional and iterative nature of transitional change, it is usually implemented through a project management process.[6] Since the old state and desired new state are both clearly known, budget, timelines, people, and other key resources can be earmarked to participate in the change. Both the starting point and desired future outcome are known,

Figure 3.2 Transitional change

so transitional change can be dealt with in an orderly, structured manner. While unexpected outcomes may occur at various points during the transition, a calculated and thorough approach minimizes such occurrences and any accompanying problems can be dealt with through the use of contingencies as accounted for within a solid plan. As such, HR professionals can display strong change management competencies and add strategic value by working with organizational leaders to ensure that the plans to move (or transition) to the new state are clearly documented and followed. Gantt charts can aid in this process and be used as a key tool for tracking progress.[7]

While planned and detailed, transitional change is not without its pitfalls and potential limitations. This type of modification is somewhat similar to using a dimmer switch to increase the lighting in a room. As the movement from darkness is transcended to brightness over a period of time with planned incremental steps (i.e., the switch is slowly turned), the light in the room eventually becomes substantially different with an entirely new environment being created. A danger of this is that people can become frustrated as the change takes time to occur and the desired outcome may not be reached as quickly and efficiently as desired. A further danger is that due to the slow and steady nature of the change, people can become confused and lack an understanding of what is actually happening or what is actually being modified. Given the need to entirely change something, a new state will eventually be created and as such, employees cannot ignore the changes or easily revert back to previous patterns of behavior, as is possible with tangential change. However, employees may not completely utilize the required changes, thereby not allowing for full benefits to be realized within the new state. Therefore, HR professionals need to be keenly aware of, and attentive to, this type of change and the resulting disinterest, frustration, and confusion that may ensue. Bored, disenchanted, and ill-informed employees, while not ignoring the change, will not fully understand or appreciate the change. As such, these employees will not utilize the change to its full potential, thereby minimizing the positive ramifications. The ability to keep people interested in, fully knowledgeable about, and engaged with, transitional change is a necessary change management competency that HR professionals should possess. Again, Chapter 4 will address ways that HR professionals can ensure that this occurs, but it is first crucial that HR professionals recognize that transitional change is occurring in order to ensure it is successful. As such, it is worthwhile to review examples of this category of change.

Examples of Transitional Change

Movement from an old state to a new state, in a deliberate and planned manner, occurs in organizations in many different ways. Think about the following list and whether your company has encountered these or similar scenarios:

- Completely new products or services are implemented to replace old ones.
- A new policy or procedure must be followed, with previous requirements being eliminated.
- Corporate restructuring or reorganizing reporting relationships.
- Replacement of a computer program or application with completely new software or a new provider.

A simple way to recognize transitional change in your organization is to think of the "out with the old, in with the new" mantra. As previously addressed, it is critical that HR professionals acknowledge and be involved in these types of amendments as they require that employees not only alter their work processes, but due to the changes to role requirements within an entirely new state, must also reconfigure their understanding of what their work involves and how to do this work. In other words, transitional change alters both an employee's actions and mind and HR professionals must ensure that people do not become confused or frustrated with, and ultimately disengaged with, the change process as evolution to the new state of being transpires over time.

Transformational Change

Transformational change is the most complex type of organizational change as it involves a radical shift in a company's mission, vision, and value systems, ultimately leading to a complete overhaul of the organization's operations.[8] This can be thought of as a complete re-engineering or reinvention of a company. An organization is altering its *raison d'être* and therefore employees need to be able to enact and embrace these amendments that strike at the very core of a company. As such, the organizational culture will need to be altered as well, involving not only how employees enact and think about their work, but also how they work with, and relate to, each other and those external to the organization. Owing to the way that an organization has to completely reconstruct itself, transformational change often alters relationships and interactions that employees have with one another as well as with customers, suppliers, competitors, and government agencies. This is a drastic modification that impacts not only what employees do, but also how they *feel* about what they do. In other words, transformational changes impact employees' hands, heads, *and* hearts. This type of amendment requires an organization to reinvent itself and the desired end state is often unknown or not fully clear as the change commences. As such, transformational change is often described with adjectives such as murky, confusing, messy, and chaotic. As Figure 3.3 indicates, in lieu of having clear and detailed plans, the move from the current state is filled with unexpected twists, turns, and course corrections as the envisioned, but not fully clear future state, is pursued. A vision for the new state exists, but this desired outcome will often evolve and alter as the change progresses with amendments to action plans and goals along the way.[9] Further, the force(s) of change is often altering and shifting, further causing the organization to alter its trajectory during this type of transformation. This is a lengthy process, often occurring over many months or even years.

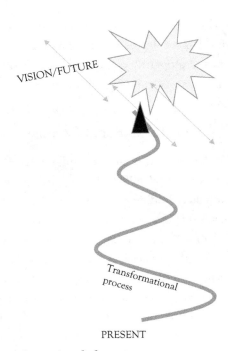

Figure 3.3 Transformational change

Transformational change can be further understood with a comparison, or analogy, to sailing. When setting out in the boat a destination is in mind, but as the winds and waters change (i.e., as the drivers of change alter), and even the desires and aspirations of the occupants alter, the sails must be adjusted in often less than ideal conditions. As well, the actual shoreline is often not within the line of sight, so faith that an actual landing spot or destination is *out there and achievable* is required. When all is said and done, the destination may not end up being exactly what was first thought (i.e., the shoreline will be reached, but it could be vastly different than the originally charted location), with numerous course corrections being made along the journey. During times of transformational change, decisions must be made, and actions taken, without full information or understanding of consequences. As such, employees are often fearful and can become paralyzed, thereby halting progress. Therefore, one critical way that HR professionals can display strong change management competencies and provide strategic value during this type of turbulent change is to ensure that progress continues and that people do not get bogged down by uncertainty and worn out by the ongoing amendments to plans and actions that are required. Given the complexity of transformational change, HR professionals must be acutely aware of, and engaged in, people's logical *and* emotive reactions to the shift that is occurring. The impactful nature of this type of change means that employees cannot ignore it or find simple and quick ways to incorporate it into their usual work patterns, as is common for tangential change. Nor can employees implement something new by merely changing their actions, skills, and understanding of their work, as needed for transitional change. Therefore, HR professionals must deal with complex, often difficult, human reactions, and not ignore or avoid these often difficult interactions in times of organizational transformation. HR professionals need to ensure that employees do not become fatigued and lose faith in the process, outcome, and the organization's leadership during this type of initiative. As previously noted, Chapter 4 will address ways that HR professionals can ensure successful transformational change, but in order to do so, HR professionals must first be aware that this is occurring.

Examples of Transformational Change

The nature of transformational change necessitates that people use, understand, and feel the repercussions of the fluctuation, as this journey involves working toward an uncertain, but better vision of the future. Think about the following list and whether your company has encountered these or similar scenarios:

- A move from focusing on accounting services to providing strategic consulting services.
- A move from offering basic banking services to supplying customer-centered investment and financial planning advice.
- A move from operating a small coffee shop to providing an Internet café where people can buy various beverages, unwind, or meet and connect with others.
- A move from supplying data encryption services to offering online payment functions.

Each of these noted examples highlights that transformational change necessitates a shift in people's understanding of the nature of the business and requires employees to have/develop new or different skills and abilities in order to work within a drastically different environment or work culture. As well, the very way employees will need to interact and relate to each other, as well as other stakeholders, and view and be inspired by the nature of their work must be altered as well. It is much more than simply understanding what has changed and involves a necessity to believe in and support the change through a readjustment to changed organizational operations, values, and beliefs. In sum, transformational change has the power to drastically modify an organization and its strategic outcomes, but HR professionals must never lose sight of the fact that this, in turn, requires that people are able to have faith to advance toward an uncertain future, thereby working and progressing during times of uncertainty while aligning with, supporting, and believing in a completely revised organization that wants to accomplish drastically different outcomes.[10]

The Interplay among Categories of Change

Tangential, transitional, and transformational organizational changes are not necessarily independent of one another. Often an amendment will involve more than one, or even all three categories of change, on some level. This is rather like the nesting Russian dolls, with tangential change being a subset of transitional change, which could also be embedded within a transformational change. Therefore, when thinking about the category of change an organization is experiencing, it is important that HR professionals are not limited or narrow in their analysis of the situation. An overly simplistic view (i.e., it is this type of change *or* that type of change) would not adequately highlight what is occurring and would therefore diminish HR professionals' understanding of how to enact change management competencies.

Summary

HR professionals must take the time to think deeply about, and understand, what category of change(s) an organizational initiative encompasses.

Time taken to fully understand and define what is occurring leads to enhanced capacity to understand the complexity of the change as well as the required time and resources. As well, key pitfalls that are typically encountered within this category of change are illuminated. As such, a thorough and deeper understanding of the type of organizational change being enacted enables HR professionals to provide proactive and strategic responses meant to guard against, or eliminate, the typical issues that derail the various categories of change. How HR professionals should respond to peoples' inconsistent application or avoidance of small changes during tangential change would be different than how HR professionals should respond to employees becoming bored and losing interest in the creation of an entirely new state during transitional change, and different yet again when stakeholders are asked to reconfigure their entire understanding of the organization's mission and the entire way of being/operating during times of transformational change. Chapter 4 therefore provides an exploration of specific change management tools and techniques, through the use of a formula for change, that HR professionals can utilize in order to best respond to the specific category of change being encountered and ensure the success of these initiatives.

End of Chapter Questions

- Think about a tangential change that your organization has experienced. Would you describe this as a successful change management initiative? Why or why not? What were your key learnings from this experience?
- Think about a transitional change that your organization has experienced. Would you describe this as a successful change management initiative? Why or why not? What were your key learnings from this experience?
- Think about a transformational change that your organization has experienced. Would you describe this as a successful change management initiative? Why or why not? What were your key learnings from this experience?
- How would you explain to a manager in your organization (in your own words) the different categories of change?

How would you help the manager understand (again in your own words) the value received from taking the time to fully understand the category of change (or changes) that is (are) occurring.

CHAPTER 4

A Formula for Managing Change

Things do not change; we change.

—Henry David Thoreau

The ability to successfully implement change means having to deal with people, while recognizing, anticipating, responding to, and valuing their reactions to the modification. Simply put, nothing will ultimately be altered if the people involved in, or affected by, the modification do not change.[1] While this may seem basic, it is often forgotten and a key reason why many changes fail or do not accomplish their full impact. Far too many change initiatives focus on *what* has to change (i.e., focus on the content of the change) while failing to acknowledge and attend to *who* has to change.[2] In all categories of change (tangential, transitional, and transformational) there are critical actions that must be taken, or issues that must be addressed, if an initiative is to be successful. While each person brings individual needs and complexities to a situation, HR professionals can still use a scientific approach to change management by attending to a critical formula that promotes successful change and achievement of lasting consequence. Given the focus on people, it may appear counterintuitive to approach change in a scientific or contrived manner, but failure to do so is what often detracts from, or completely dismantles, change initiatives.

The change management formula, which addresses change in a scientific or more prescribed manner, focuses on four key areas: Dissatisfaction with the status quo, Vision, Steps and Resistance.[3] As indicated in Figure 4.1, the first three elements influence each other and when accounted for in summation, must outweigh or be greater than encountered resistance.[4]

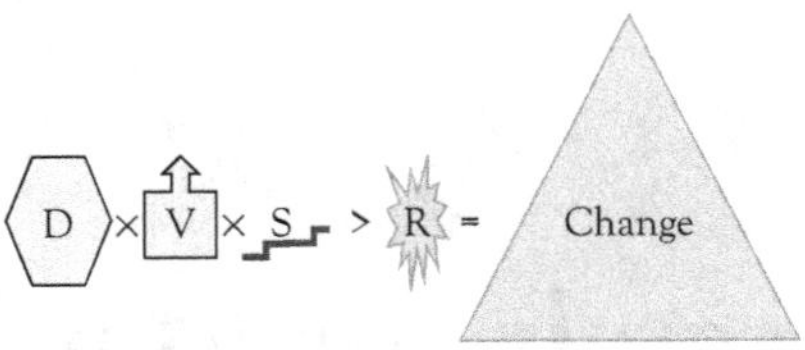

Figure 4.1 A formula for managing change

Each element within the formula, and its specific applications during various categories of change, enable HR professionals to effectively guide and facilitate organizational change initiatives, thereby providing strategic value within, and to, an organization. As such, exploration of the elements within the change formula and how HR professionals can utilize them during different categories of change is warranted.

Increasing Dissatisfaction with the Status Quo

Increasing dissatisfaction may, at first glance, appear to be a counterintuitive approach to dealing with change. Why would an HR professional want to stir up and invoke negative thoughts and feelings? The simple answer is that people are creatures of habit and tend to want and support change only when they realize that the continuation of the current situation, or the status quo, no longer meets their needs or desires and/or is in some manner detrimental to them. People need to realize that the same old processes and procedures will no longer suffice and without change poor outcomes will ensue. Many people subscribe to the belief that "if it ain't broke don't fix it." As an example, a person will not take his car to a mechanic to have specialized work performed (this is not referring to regular or expected ongoing maintenance such as an oil change) if it is functioning properly. Taking action to alter the vehicle and have parts replaced and repaired, when everything appears to be working properly, is seen as a waste of time, energy, and money.

By illuminating why the status quo is no longer tenable or desirable, HR professionals are, in essence, showing that the current circumstances are in fact *broken* and are no longer acceptable or viable. Further, as part of understanding that the status quo is no longer acceptable, people need to realize why and how this impacts them. This is also known as a WIFM, or what's in it for me? In order for change to occur people need to feel personal, and negative consequence, if a situation remains stagnant. Continuing with the previous example, this is rather like the *check engine light* appearing, signaling that the current situation is no longer working and that something within the vehicle needs to change.

So, how can the HR professionals illuminate the check engine light, per se, within organizations? A key part of increasing dissatisfaction with the status quo is doing so in a manner that does not use threats or fear mongering. This is not a simple task and not only *what* is said to increase dissatisfaction, but also *how* the information or messaging is conveyed is of vital importance. When asked to get others to see that a situation is no longer acceptable, it is common to use intimidation or anxiety to invoke change. Comments such as "if you do not change you will lose your job" or "if things do not improve we will be bankrupt" only serve to incite panic or despair, with the typical response of people shutting off and ultimately resisting change. This is rather akin to shouting at someone whose engine light is on and telling them that their car will explode and they will face certain death if something is not fixed and changed. Or, this is rather like an alarm sounding as the light continues to blink off and on. This only serves to annoy someone, who will ultimately find a way to ignore these cues or will find a way to shut them off in order to avoid the warnings. This type of dramatic, exaggerated, and fear-inducing request to attend to change is typically met with a belief that the person requesting the change really does not know what is going on, is paranoid, or is exaggerating the urgency of the situation and that there really is no need to change. Again, threats and fear do not promote change. Instead, they typically incite people to ignore, avoid, dismiss, or shut down altogether.[5]

Therefore, dissatisfaction with the status quo must be created in a calm and well thought-out manner and by helping people realize that the current situation is no longer working and is causing them problems and/or that changes will ultimately result in a better circumstance for them. This should be done with the use of facts or evidence in a logical and nonintimidating fashion. Examples of how to do this include sharing statistics and metrics, providing proof of changed requirements through legislation or altered industry standards, sharing of consumer feedback/requests, and demonstration of how changes have brought about success for other organizations, also known as benchmarking. Thinking about the specific driver of change often points to or leads to ways to increase dissatisfaction with the status quo, as evidence of the required alteration is pronounced within the force behind the modification. For example, if legislative requirements are driving a change, then the details and communication around this should be shared with employees. Or, if customer requirements are the driving force, then evidence of changing customer needs, through feedback obtained, should be shared.

Using the example of the engine light, it would be best to increase someone's dissatisfaction with the status quo by showing them research demonstrating that lack of attention to a malfunctioning engine only serves to create other costly mechanical problems or providing evidence showing the consequence of poor gas mileage when a car is not operating correctly. Helping people realize that the current situation is not providing them with the best possible circumstances and that other negative consequences could ensue as well, without using alarming or terrifying tactics, is fundamental to increasing dissatisfaction with the status quo and triggering a key element within the change formula. Simply put, increasing dissatisfaction with the status quo addresses *why this change is really needed.*

Understanding the need to increase dissatisfaction with the status quo allows for implementation of actions within each type of change that help negate the prevalent pitfalls (as addressed in Chapter 3) that occur within each category. Again, it must be stressed that these tactics to increase dissatisfaction with the status quo must rely on facts, evidence, and logic and *not* be seen as threats or based upon creating fear. HR professionals can therefore utilize this competency within each category of change.

Dissatisfaction and Tangential Change

Discontent with the status quo must show people that even minor or apparently inconsequential processes, rules, actions, products, and/or services are taking away from success in their roles. It must be displayed that even small changes will have impact and therefore allow people's work to be easier or more gratifying. By showing people that their current situation is taking away from their enjoyment and accomplishments, and that this could be rectified by minor alterations, an increase in dissatisfaction with the status quo will be created and enticement to embrace, consistently use, and maintain tangential changes will be created.

Dissatisfaction and Transitional Change

Discontent with the status quo must show that the current state of operations is no longer meeting needs (i.e., customer desires, legislative requirements, and ability to meet or beat competitors) and that without change, the organization will not succeed and may eventually be unable to operate at all. It must be clearly shown that the current situation is no longer tenable and that processes and/or services and/or products need to entirely change in order to ensure the ongoing success of the organization. This type of understanding of why things cannot remain as they are helps to prevent boredom and frustration during the progress to the new state.

Dissatisfaction and Transformational Change

Discontent with the status quo during times of transformational change is very similar to the strategy used for transitional change, except the scope is larger. It must be shown that the current state of the company and its operational goals (i.e., not just specific processes, services or products) needs to completely change. Through the use of evidence, facts and logic, a deeper understanding of why things cannot remain the same is created and therefore the emotive and often difficult human reactions, such as lack of belief and faith in the value of the amendment, to transformational change are better addressed and dealt with.

While increasing dissatisfaction with the status quo must be enacted across all categories of change, so too must increasing the vision, and this is addressed as the second element within the formula for managing change.

Increasing the Vision

In addition to increasing unhappiness with the current state of affairs, it is also critical to create an enhanced vision of what the change will create. Dissatisfaction with the status quo addresses the now and increasing vision addresses the future. Knowing the end state, or what the consequence of the change will be, helps provide a beacon and guide to people. Picturing what could be, in lieu of what currently is, will provide possibilities and promises of better outcomes, which is required in order for successful change to occur.[6] This is rather like using the picture on a puzzle box to complete the task. Having an understanding of the desired result helps to drive people forward, provides inspiration, enhances motivation and helps stimulate ongoing engagement with the change process along the way. Again, using the check engine light analogy, this would involve telling someone how enjoyable the driving experience could be by creating a picture, through deep and vivid descriptions, of what it would be like to operate a fully functioning car that is not encountering mechanical issues. The idea of a smooth ride, free of worries and distractions, must reside in the automobile owner in order to know why bothering with the change is worthwhile. A compelling vision not only provides a visual impetus, but allows someone to *feel* what it would be like to be in the new environment, thereby appealing to both logical and emotive influences. Chapter 8 will address communication during times of change and how best to enact these types of responses from key stakeholders. Simply put, increasing the vision addresses what the purpose of this change is by providing a deeply desirable goal and end state and should be addressed within each category of change.

Vision and Tangential Change

Through increasing the vision, people are motivated to use and sustain even small changes, as the desired results are seen to be worthwhile. As such, the likelihood of inconsistent application, avoidance, and/or return to previous patterns or ways of doing things is less likely. An understanding of how incremental changes can ultimately provide a desirable outcome is critical within tangential change. The vision must clearly depict how incremental amendments, even though appearing to be inconsequential, actually lead to important alterations and beneficial results.

Vision and Transitional Change

As the move from the current state to a new state transpires, people who are captivated by a vibrant and motivating picture of the new reality are less likely to become bored or disinterested with the process. An enticing goal keeps people focused and engaged with the change process itself. Further, a clear and compelling vision helps develop an understanding that the desired new state is both feasible and desirable. As such, boredom and frustration are minimized and people are also more likely to fully utilize the changes in the new state, in order to completely realize the benefits of the altered circumstances.

Vision and Transformational Change

Increasing the vision during transformational change takes skillful and ongoing communication, as the desired end state is not fully known and is ever evolving. In order to fully recognize and respond to people's powerful and emotive reactions, transparent and honest information must be strategically planned and shared with ongoing updates given as the ultimate vision becomes clearer. In order to minimize negative emotive responses, and consequent derailment of the transformational change, initial communication should fully convey what the current vision is and be clear that this desired end state will be evolving as the change progresses. As well, the vision must be amended as the force(s) for change requires shifts in the required outcome. It is also then necessary to provide timely and regular updates as the vision for the desired end state becomes clearer. This honest and candid sharing of the vision, on a continuing basis, will help ensure the success of the sought-after change, as it helps to increase the faith that people have that the final state will be desirable and is achievable.

While increasing dissatisfaction with the status quo addresses the *now*, and increasing the vision addresses the *future*, attention to the required process *or the path from the now to the future* is dealt with by attending to the steps within the change process, which is the third element within the formula for managing change.

Attending to the Steps

While an understanding that the status quo is not tenable and having a vision of the desired result are important, it is also critical that the *process* of change be acknowledged and celebrated. As such, steps should be viewed as the operational plan for change and should show the details of how to move away from the undesirable current state to the envisioned new outcome. This is rather akin to the famous saying that "those who fail to plan should plan to fail." Having concrete action plans, or steps, in place shows employees that the change has been well thought out and there is commitment from the organization's leadership to actually implement and support the change. This minimizes the view that the desired change is just a passing fad or will soon be forgotten. In other words, a well-planned strategy legitimizes and enhances the change management process. Further, some view this element of the change management formula as giving special attention to, and planning for, the first concrete steps. As such, the formula for managing change typically is expressed by acknowledging the importance of attending to, or increasing focus on, the first steps toward a desired change. While all steps in the process are important, in order for a change to gain momentum it is of utmost importance that the first movements toward the change are tangible, and highly visible and promoted, thereby showing employees that the change is to be taken seriously.[7]

As well, when critical steps along the change process have been achieved it is important to recognize and acknowledge this. Celebrating accomplishment of key steps does not have to involve a lot of money or energy. The mere act of taking time to acknowledge achievement of steps helps to once again legitimize the planned change and maintain employees' momentum and commitment to the change. In other words, employees believe that if effort is made to actually recognize and reward key milestones within the change process, then there is true organizational commitment and support for the change and desire to ensure that it actually transpires and is maintained. Celebrating steps can be enacted in many ways, ranging from a sincere verbal *thank you,* to e-mails announcing and acknowledging key results, to a sponsored lunch to a token of appreciation (monetary or otherwise), to acknowledging results as part of the formal performance management process. The key issue is that employees know that the organization's leadership is actually aware of the successes that are being accomplished to advance the change and that this matters enough to be appreciated (i.e., that the leadership team truly cares about this).

Again, using the engine light example, this would involve having a plan in place of how to rectify the problem. Details could involve the following: research possible mechanics, call for quotes, select best option, book the appointment, and go to the appointment. At key points, or steps, in this process it would be advisable to plan a way to celebrate progress toward the end goal. So, after an appointment is booked, a person could reward himself/herself by purchasing a treat, and at the appointment while waiting for the car a special coffee could be purchased. While these might appear to be rather trivial or inconsequential actions, having rewards, no matter how minor, in place at key stages along a process does in fact help to drive the change forward and make those involved in the change to feel better about what is transpiring. It is interesting to note that when people are trying to invoke changes in their own lives (i.e., like trying to ensure that they make time to have their automobile fixed) small rewards, even if provided by themselves, actually do help to ensure that the changes occur.

Given the criticality of attending to the steps within change management, an exploration of how to enact this within various categories of change is warranted.

Steps and Tangential Change

Given the minor, and often quick nature of tangential change, it is easy to believe that there is no requirement to plan the steps toward the desired outcome. To borrow from a popular slogan, it is thought that people should "just do it" and the new outcome, whether it be a service, process, or product, should just be invoked. In other words, the change should just be implemented and used without any fuss. However, even the most minor changes can, and should, be broken down into smaller steps toward the end goal. For example, training is usually provided to employees to assist with even minor changes. Completion of such development provides a tremendous opportunity to acknowledge and recognize achievement of a key step within the change process. Moreover, recognition of how employees are actively trying to use the change (i.e., use the new process, deliver the new product or service) is part of celebrating key steps. Again, it must be stressed that these *celebrations* can be as simple as verbal acknowledgment and gratitude, corporate announcements of progress achieved to date, or low-cost rewards ranging from free donuts to lunch. The key point is that progress, even though it may seem inconsequential, toward the desired end state is both recognized and valued. It is important to remember that even a small change contains micro changes within it, and it is critical to plan for ways to acknowledge and celebrate achievement of key points along the way. Doing so helps to ensure consistent and continuous application of the desired change and prevents employees from forgetting about or ignoring the change altogether.

Steps and Transitional Change

By the very nature of transitional change movement from the old state to the desired new state can be implemented through a project management, or very intentional, process. As previously noted, desired steps along the change process as well as achievement and responsibility for these steps, can be tracked through the use of Gantt charts. It is therefore beneficial to include deliberate ways to recognize and acknowledge accomplishments at key junctures within the process. In other words, these celebrations can be documented and planned for within the plans or Gantt charts. This ensures that people do not become bored, disinterested, or disengaged during the change process. As well, celebration of key milestones ensures that employees continue to receive information about the change and its progress, thereby further advancing the initiative. Again, it must be stressed that these celebrations do not have to be elaborate but should be appropriate for the achievement. Examples include e-mail or intranet announcements of success achieved to date, presentation of gift cards, coffee and cake events, and personalized thank you notes to employees. The key point is that attention to steps enhances buy-in and keeps people on track with, engaged with and supportive of the transitional change, thereby increasing the likelihood of a successful outcome and full, ongoing utilization of the change once the new state is achieved.

Steps and Transformational Change

Owing to the evolutionary nature of transformational change, attention to, and recognition of, steps within the process can be quite complicated.

Given the mutable nature of these initiatives, people often believe that time and energy spent planning is ill-advised. However, proposed actions should still be put in place and monitored. The key point is that plans will have to be altered and adjusted as the process unfolds, but to avoid planning altogether due to the uncertainty associated within this type of change is harmful. Drafting of a tentative plan sets a course for the change process and helps to signal when amendments to the process need to be made and acknowledged. As with alterations to the vision during times of transformation, so too must the steps be amended to adjust to ongoing shifts brought about by evolution within the change driver, or drivers, themselves.

Further, through acknowledgment and recognition that achievement of critical points in the process is occurring, even if these have been revised since the change initially began, people are better able to have faith that the change is actually progressing and that while not fully defined, movement toward the future is indeed occurring and the process is evolving as it should.

Given that transformational change involves a complete overhaul of an organization, celebrations at key junctures in the process, while not needing to be elaborate or expensive, should be across the entire organization. By ensuring that all employees receive acknowledgment (e.g., through e-mails, announcements, compensation, or events) at the same time, indication is given to everyone that the organization is changing and advancing in a new direction. Consistent and continued reinforcement at key stages during the change helps employees to maintain faith that things are progressing as they should and that the future organization, while vastly different than what was previously known, is indeed achievable.

Resistance

The final element within the formula for managing change addresses resistance. Another way to understand this is to examine why people will likely struggle with change. As noted in Figure 4.2, Mauer addressed three key areas of resistance known as personal, intellectual, and core. Each of these levels of resistance is more tangible within various categories of change.[8] As previously noted, a common pitfall within tangential change is that people may inconsistently apply/incorporate the change or may

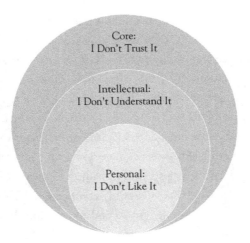

Figure 4.2 Key areas of resistance

ignore it altogether. This may be described as personal level resistance, or thought of as employees thinking "I do not like this change." Boredom and frustration with transitional change, as well as a lack of information during and about the process, can lead to an intellectual level of resistance, which may be thought of as employees thinking "I do not understand this change." Transformational change strikes at the very heart of organizations and employees, and due to the need to alter values and beliefs in addition to the entire operations and focus of an organization, this addresses a core level of resistance or may be thought of as employees thinking "I do not trust this change."

Just as the categories of change are embedded in each other and may be found in various change initiatives, so too are the types of resistance. For example, a change initiative may have elements of tangential change within a transitional change, thereby highlighting key points of resistance at both personal and intellectual levels. Or, a transformational change may have elements of transitional and tangential change, thereby necessitating acknowledgment of personal, intellectual, and core resistance levels. Therefore, effective and thoughtful utilization of increasing dissatisfaction with the status quo, increasing the vision, and attending to and celebrating steps within the change process will address each of these key resistance levels, thereby minimizing or eliminating potential derailment of the entire change initiative.

While each type of change has typical pitfalls, or key resistance issues, there are numerous and overlapping reasons across all categories of change regarding why people will resist. Understanding key resistance factors will enable HR professionals to plan how to avoid or lessen these detractors during the change management process. Therefore, enhancing the three elements within the formula for managing change (dissatisfaction with the status quo, vision, and steps) is important, but so is finding strategic ways to reduce overall resistance to any type of change.[9] As shown in the formula (see Figure 4.1), lowering encountered opposition will better enable the combination, or total effect, of the other three factors to work together to overcome resistance to change. Therefore, attention to resistance and how to avoid or minimize it is a critical change management competency for HR professionals and is the focus of Chapter 5.

Summary

Change management will be enhanced through the use of a formula that addresses key elements within any change initiative. Increasing dissatisfaction with the status quo can be seen as referring to *why* the change is needed. Increasing the vision addresses *what* the desired end result is and steps attend to *how* the change will be accomplished. The goal is to have these three aforementioned factors, when enhanced in conjunction with each other, act as a greater force in support of change than the encountered resistance to the change. In other words, when working together and influencing each other, these three factors must be greater than the resistance to the desired change. While there are common pitfalls or resistance factors that are prevalent within each category of change, there are also prevailing reasons that people resist all categories of change and these issues need to be addressed, prevented, and/or minimized as part of effective change management. This is the focus of Chapter 5.

End of Chapter Questions

Think about a change* that you are currently experiencing or have recently experienced. This can be a professional or personal example.

- How effectively was dissatisfaction with the status quo increased? What would you do (could you do) differently to enhance this without using threats or fear? What specific resources enable a better understanding of why the current situation is/was no longer acceptable?
- How effectively was increasing of the vision enacted? What would you do (could you do) differently to enhance this? Did you have (do you have) a solid understanding of the vision yourself? Why or why not?
- How effectively were the steps attended to, including celebrating accomplishment of key milestones along the process? What would you do (could you do) differently to better focus on the change journey and successes along the way?

Note: Think about a tangential, transitional, and transformational change that you are experiencing or have experienced and repeat these questions for each category of change.

CHAPTER 5

Resistance to Change

People don't resist change. They resist being changed.

—Peter Senge

Helping people to embrace and enact change by increasing dissatisfaction with the status quo, increasing the vision about the desired outcome, and using planned steps and celebrating accomplishment of key milestones during the process are necessary, but the desired change will not be as impactful, beneficial, or long-lasting if people are ultimately opposed to the change itself. Therefore, attention to key issues that block or detract from change is necessary.[1] With knowledge of why people typically resist change, these factors can be avoided, or at least minimized, during any change initiative. As such, understanding the reasons behind people's resistance to change is the first step to minimizing or avoiding it. The ability to do this allows HR professionals to provide needed and valued change management expertise.

A Sense of Loss

When people typically think of change, their first reaction is to envision what they have to give up in order to accommodate the amendment. This is a natural human reaction. For most people, change equals the loss of something.[2] In lieu of envisioning and appreciating what is to be gained as a result of change, the usual response is to focus on, and fret about, what will be taken away. While the level and depth of worry can, and will, alter based upon the nature and type of the change, it is expected that people will anticipate loss, with some intensity, across any and all changes. Even during what is thought to be *good or positive change*, people will still experience loss. Think about graduation from school or the start of a new job. People typically view these occasions as positive things, but the loss of previous roles (i.e., I am no longer a student or I am no longer an employee of my previous company) still should be acknowledged and honored. It is a noted phenomenon that people rarely recognize their sense of loss overtly when a constructive change is occurring, as the focus tends to be only on the positive occurrences and outcomes.[3] This, in turn, actually can diminish the benefits realized from what is viewed as a positive change, as resistance is not expected, acknowledged, or properly dealt with. Or, what someone may view as a positive change another person, based upon perception, values, and goals, may think of as a negative occurrence. As such, honoring, respecting, and expecting peoples' sense of loss during what is labeled as either negative or positive change is essential.

It is also critical to note that peoples' perceptions are important. While there actually may not be any loss, if people believe and feel there is, then there is.[4] To borrow from the marketing mantra, "perception is reality." This is important, because when people believe they are facing loss due to a change, and focus on this loss, resistance increases. In contrast, when worry about loss can be negated or minimized the negative impact of resistance is, in turn, lessened. As such, key issues that people are apprehensive about during times of change need to be acknowledged along and strategic responses to these concerns need to be implemented. One method of doing so is to examine the shifting nature of power dynamics during times of change.

The Connection between Power and Loss

When change occurs the processes and networks that people utilize to accomplish their tasks and interact with others are typically altered as well. A common outcome of these amendments is an accompanying change in peoples' control, or power over, key issues and/or factors within an organization, including but not limited to their own jobs. As such, the elements within French and Raven's sources of power model can be used as a method to better understand people's sense of loss during times of change and ways to minimize these concerns regarding perceived deficits.[5]

Coercive Power

The ability or authority to invoke punishment or negative consequences upon others is known as coercive power.[6] Organizational examples include docking pay, giving a poor performance rating or denying requests for certain shifts or vacation time. While coercive power is not viewed as the best form of control to ultimately bring about lasting results, loyalty and true employee engagement, it is nonetheless a source of control that people do use in organizations. As such, people worry that organizational change may result in diminished authority and responsibility for them, thereby taking away the power they hold over others. This form of loss is something that people will be concerned about and will therefore work against change if it means that they will no longer be able to exert this type of control over negative consequences that can be allocated to others.

As well, during times of change people may worry about modifications to those who have coercive power over them. Possible changes to the authority given to others (i.e., through alterations to reporting relationships and organizational structure), necessitated and/or brought about by the changes being implemented, could result in new and different people having the power to negatively impact others and this too is a source of concern and worry for people. Further, people are concerned with equity and fairness. When there is a change in those who control negative repercussions, concern exists that the workplace may alter its approach to justice and equal treatment. As such, people worry that changes may result in them receiving poorer treatment than they previously did prior to the change.

Reward Power

In contrast to coercive power, reward power is the ability that someone has to provide positive outcomes, or incentives, to another person.[7] This could involve paying bonuses, allocating desirable projects, providing coveted working space, and granting favors such as time off. During times of organizational change, it is typical for people to worry that their position will no longer hold the same level of influence within the company's hierarchy and that this could result in a diminished capacity to provide positive outcomes or incentives to others. Just as with coercive power, this form of loss is something that people will be concerned about and will therefore work against change if it means that they will no longer be able to exert this type of control over positive outcomes.

Also, as with coercive power, during times of change people may worry about modifications to those who have reward power over them. Possible changes to the authority given to others, necessitated and/or brought about by the changes being implemented, could result in new and different people having power to positively impact others and this too is a source of concern and worry for people. As with coercive power, when there is a change in those who control allocation of rewards, concern exists that the workplace may alter its approach to justice and equal treatment. As such, people worry that changes may result in them receiving poorer treatment, such as fewer rewards or less desirable rewards, than they previously did before the change was implemented.

Expert Power

When people possess knowledge or skills that are required and valued by others, this is known as expert power.[8] However, an organizational change may necessitate that people's roles be altered, thereby causing revisions to specific elements within various functions throughout a company. As requirements change, it is common for people to worry that they will not be able to keep up with the needed changes, or that other people will become more knowledgeable and competent based upon changing conditions, and therefore they will no longer be viewed as the *go to person* or authority regarding various issues. This, in turn, leaves people with a diminished sense of value, as they are no longer seen as the authority that others turn to for advice, guidance, and expertise.

Whether it be small amendments or major additions or completely new tasks within a company, the shift in requirements equates to a new way of having to work. This often leaves people with concern that they may no longer be competent in their roles. People worry that their reputation as an expert will suffer if they cannot competently fulfill the requirements of their jobs. A great deal of peoples' identities are linked to their roles and when they believe that they will no longer be able to effectively perform their work, this attacks their sense of accomplishment and purpose—the very core of their identity.[9] Further, a loss of expert power attacks peoples' sense of security. When confronted with a loss in their ability to effectively perform their role, concern over negative performance feedback, diminished pay increases, disciplinary action, and even ultimately termination from the role can occur. A loss of expert power, due to the changes being implemented, therefore strikes peoples' sense of stability and control over their own destiny and future opportunities. As such, resistance to change in an attempt to avoid these concerns can be expected.

Legitimate Power

Legitimate power is obtained due to the position that a person holds.[10] By the very nature of the role within a company's organizational structure, certain positions have authority to make decisions, control resources, and direct the work of others. During times of organizational change it is typical for people to worry that their position will no longer hold the same level of influence within the company's hierarchy and that this will result in diminished authority and responsibility. Again, this leaves people with a diminished sense of importance, as they are no longer able to exert the same amount of control and regulation over the work environment. This, in turn, provides another source of resistance to change.

Informational Power

There is a familiar saying that "information is power." This statement conveys that those who control, or have access to, valued information are seen to hold power and influence over others.[11] In the roles people occupy they often have access to information as their legitimate power gives them informational power as well, but very often people find ways to access information that is not necessarily associated with their position in a company. Through developing relationships, or knowing where to look for information, or devising ways to access information, people place themselves in a position of power over others. Further, by deciding how and when information will be shared, and with whom it will be distributed, further power is achieved. People require a sense of order and control and disruption to patterns of information exchange can be alarming and disconcerting. During times of change, due to changing work patterns and relationships with others, informational power can therefore be lost or diminished. As such, concern over being left out of the loop, or lacking required information, or no longer being a source of news and updates can occur. Therefore, the fear of losing access to, and power over the distribution of, information is something that people worry about during times of change.

Referent Power

Referent power is also known as charismatic power. This type of effect on others is based upon how well someone is liked, how they develop their interpersonal connections, and how much they are respected by others.[12] People are typically concerned that organizational changes will alter their working relationships and patterns of interaction with others, thereby removing the associations that they have worked so hard to establish and develop. Further, people value and need a sense of belonging and connection to others. Being part of a group and being included and valued by others is a core human need.[13] When change involves having to work with entirely new people, the respect and admiration from others who have been previously established are eliminated and the process of developing interpersonal relationships with different people has to begin anew. The resulting loss of established interpersonal relationships and patterns, and the accompanying loss of respect from others, is a source of worry and concern during times of change.

Further, as previously noted, people gain a sense of identity and pride from their work. In other words, people like to be respected and valued for what they accomplish.[14] When the ability to achieve results is threatened due to the changes being implemented, it is much more than the work itself that is harmed. The very core of people's sense of self and sense of worth are threatened as well.

This diminished sense of self and value can be seen across perceived loss of any and all types of power, thereby helping to illuminate the various reasons why people are resistant to change. It is important to recognize that increases in power, too, can be problematic for people during times of change. Increased responsibilities for distributing punishment or rewards, enhanced access to information, enlarged responsibility within a position, and intensified expert and referent power are also possible when changes occur. These are not necessarily welcome amendments or increased obligations that people desire. People may be just as concerned, or even more concerned, about increased power that they are not willing to have, qualified to have, or interested to have. Through this lens an undesired gain, such as an increase in tasks, authority or responsibility, can actually be perceived as a form of loss. As such, with this understanding and in order to fully understand resistance points during times of change, it is perhaps better to think about both losses *and* gains to power that can be encountered during times of change, and the resulting resistance that these may cause. It is therefore important to examine how to minimize concerns regarding altered power, as this will then avoid or at least lower peoples' resistance to change.

Lowering Resistance

As noted within the formula for managing change, resistance is a key factor that must be addressed and accounted for during any change initiative. As such, lowering or minimizing resistance is one way to help ensure successful enactment and maintenance of desired change. Based on an understanding of key points of resistance, as detailed in the previous sections within this chapter, strategic ways to anticipate, eliminate, and/or lessen resistance can now be reviewed.

Training and Development

One strategic way to address resistance is to ensure that people receive training and development opportunities during change initiatives. People must clearly be told, and must fully understand, that they will receive training regarding any required amendments to the skills, knowledge, and abilities required to be effective in their roles. In addition to receiving training, people must know that they will be given time to learn and implement the newly required competencies. Opportunities to learn and develop help to lessen concerns regarding loss of expert and referent power through the ability to grow into and with the changing requirements, thereby retaining the capacity to effectively fulfill role expectations. In order to provide people with the appropriate training and development opportunities, a thorough understanding of required changes in their positions must be obtained. As such, thorough analysis of amendments to roles during times of change must occur.

Role Analysis and Requirements

During change initiatives it is critical to ensure a careful review and understanding of what, if any, changes to various jobs or roles may ensue. Therefore, updated analysis should be done to confirm complete understanding of alterations to the work being performed. A thorough understanding of what is needed in order to accomplish the required tasks can help avoid many problems that occur due to confusion over role requirements and responsibilities. This point needs to be stressed. Clear understanding of, and communication about, what is and is not required within various roles helps people understand what they are required to do as well as what they can expect from other people based upon allocation of responsibilities. Knowledge of these expectations helps to address resistance brought about by changes to key forms of power. For example, this allows for enhanced understanding of who is doing specific work, who can distribute rewards and punishment, who has access to information, and who is most knowledgeable about certain issues. Clear understanding, and communication, pertaining to the work that is performed reduces questions about authority and responsibility levels, thereby minimizing confusion or misunderstandings regarding what various roles do, or do not, involve.

It is also crucial to ensure that constructive dismissal does not inadvertently occur due to decreases in job responsibilities or the *overall level* of the job. When employees know that careful attention has been given to understand, plan for, and then communicate changing role requirements, there is less likelihood of resistance to these modifications. When it can be shown that, overall, the level of work that people perform in their roles has remained unchanged, this not only negates potential negative legal ramifications but also addresses concerns pertaining to loss of coercive, reward, informational, and legitimate power. Further, a thorough understanding of what is expected from people in their jobs helps to minimize or prevent overwork, resulting in a more even distribution of work and lessening the chance of people becoming frustrated, resentful, or burning out. As well, careful role analysis can also properly respond to increases in requirements through appropriate amendments to compensation, job descriptions, performance expectations, and so on. Changing role requirements must therefore align with other HR systems in order to properly address resistance points.

Alignment of HR Processes

Resistance to change can also be lessened by ensuring that an organization's HR processes align with and support the required amendments. As such, changes to organizational roles should not be approached with a silo mentality. Changes to requirements are accompanied by appropriate amendments to the compensation system, performance management system, reward and recognition offerings, training and development opportunities (as noted previously), and recruitment and selection processes. Simply put, HR professionals must ensure that changes to roles are supported and reinforced by alterations to other processes. This, in turn, enhances the relevance and meaning of the required changes. Changes to role requirements that are reinforced through changes in compensation, evaluation of performance, provision of rewards, opportunities for training, and how the positions are filled signals that the changes are being reinforced and supported. Doing so lessens resistance based upon concerns relating to all forms of power. While this attends to operational aspects of change, human interactions and interpersonal relationships must be addressed as well.

Attending to Interpersonal Relationships

Another way to address resistance is to recognize and respond to changing work configurations or interfaces with others. Alterations to role requirements often necessitate changes to patterns of interaction with others and as such, opportunities to get to know and develop a rapport with new people are critical. Through team building, informal events or planned meetings, opportunities for people to get to know those they work with are important. Addressing the interpersonal aspects of work helps to minimize concerns pertaining to referent power and how this can be maintained and/or enhanced during times of change. In order for people to look up to and respect one another, they need to know what it is that other people do, but also must know a little bit about who their colleagues are beyond a superficial level. Referent power has an interpersonal element to it and opportunities for people to get to know their colleagues must not be forgotten during times of change.

Communication

In order to minimize resistance during times of change ongoing communication is critical. Any plans and efforts to minimize resistance to change will be futile if people are not aware of, and fully understand, what actions are being taken and why these measures are being implemented. Communication pertaining to training and development opportunities, role analysis, and requirements, how HR processes will also change to support and align with the new work requirements and how people will have opportunities to get to know their new coworkers is critical. Communication also helps to ensure that people are involved in, both early and throughout, the change initiative, thereby further lessening their concerns and resistance. As such, two-way communication must be enabled to provide opportunities for difficult, often uncomfortable messages to be exchanged. People must feel safe expressing their resistance or concerns, and be given responses and feedback, if communication is truly to be effective.

The role and criticality of strategic communication during times of change is so significant that this topic, and techniques to enact effective messaging, will specifically be discussed and explored in Chapter 8.

While lowering resistance through various mechanisms, as outlined in this chapter, is a critical component to effective change management, the possible benefits of resistance need to be addressed as well.

The Benefits of Resistance

While minimizing, or lowering, resistance is a critical element within the formula for managing change, it is unreasonable and unrealistic to believe that all forms and types of opposition can be eliminated during times of change. As such, in lieu of dreading and condemning resistance, it is beneficial to remember that at some level, resistance may actually be used as a mechanism to enhance the enactment and maintenance of change.[15] This necessitates that signals and indication of resistance are both acknowledged and then responded to. The following are examples of how this can be accomplished:

- Resistance indicates that people have recognized that the change is occurring and are not simply ignoring it. Points of resistance can aid in the exploration and deeper understanding of the various ways that forms of power are being altered and how best to respond to this. As such, investigating resistance and engaging in further examination of it can ultimately advance the change initiative.
- Resistance can point out omissions and gaps in the plans for and the implementation of change. Using this information the steps can be altered to better ensure success.
- Resistance can delay the implementation of change, thereby allowing people the chance to catch up, adjust, and obtain the necessary skills and resources to support the change.
- Resistance can provide the chance for people to express concerns, feel involved, and reduce anxiety or feelings of loss. When given opportunities to express concerns, people will not feel ignored or devalued. This will be further explored in Chapter 8 when reviewing the importance of strategic communication during times of change.

Through a lens of viewing disapproval as a positive way to enhance the enactment and maintenance of change, resistance can in fact be used as a move toward change as opposed to against it. The issue is that too much resistance can ultimately stifle change, while an appropriate amount, when acknowledged and used strategically to respond to and enhance the change initiative, can actually be beneficial. There is no magic cut-off point to establish this delicate balance or tipping point. Instead, what is required is careful evaluation of the situation and thoughtful reaction to how people are responding to and resisting change. The ideas and concepts explored within this chapter serve to enhance the ability to do this.

Summary

Anticipating, recognizing, and responding to resistance is a key competency within effective change management. Ignoring or avoiding peoples' opposition can ultimately outweigh other efforts to enhance change management (increasing dissatisfaction with the status quo, increasing vision and attending to steps in the process), thereby eventually derailing or diminishing the change initiative. Viewing change as a form of loss of various forms of power (or unwanted gains in various forms of power) helps illuminate why and how opposition to change may be encountered. With this knowledge, appropriate actions can be implemented to anticipate, remove, or lessen resistance. Further, understanding these points of opposition can also be used to enhance change initiatives by using the signals of disapproval as indicators of issues that must continue to be addressed.

Given that the various components within the formula for managing change have now been reviewed and discussed, attention can now be directed toward how to launch change initiatives. This is the focus of Chapter 6.

End of Chapter Questions

- Why do you think people typically view change as a form of loss? What have been your own experiences with this, both personally and professionally?
- Think about a positive or good change that you have experienced, either personally or professionally. Can you articulate how this contained a component of loss, even though it was perceived to be, or labeled, as a positive event?
- Think about a change (personal or professional) that you have recently experienced. What forms of power were altered during this process? Did you experience personal resistance based on this, and if so, how was this resistance shown? Did you witness other peoples' resistance, and if so, how did they

express this? Think about both losses and unwanted gains as forms of alteration to power.
- Using the change you thought of for the previously noted questions, which of the ideas shared in this chapter could you use to lower resistance?
- Review the list of possible benefits of resistance to change. What other benefits could you envision would be brought about from resistance?

CHAPTER 6

Launching Change

The beginning is the most important part.

—Plato

Equipped with an understanding of the driving force(s) behind a change, the type of change(s) being addressed and how to effectively utilize the formula for managing change, it is then necessary to initiate a change. As the saying goes, "you only get one chance to make a first impression." So it is with the commencement of change as well. Only one opportunity is given to begin and this should be viewed as a form of impression management. As such, *how* a change is started will impact how effective and lasting the change ultimately is. When properly begun, a change can excite and unite people toward the desired end state. In contrast, an ineffective beginning will only serve to confuse and discourage people, thereby turning them off and away from the sought-after outcome.

The manner in which a change is launched is something that people will not quickly forget. As such, commencement not only affects the change at hand, but also has implications on future projects.[1] Lack of success with a current change launch detracts from future achievements in this regard, as there is concern that any subsequent actions are merely more of the same old rhetoric and people worry that if it did not work in the past, why would it this time? In contrast, a successful start to a change initiative serves to build confidence, as people believe that if things could begin effectively in the past, then this could be accomplished again in future change endeavors. As such, a current project could actually be thwarted, or enhanced, due to previous encounters and experiences that people have had with the start of an organization's other change initiatives. Therefore, how a change is started has implication beyond the present focus, as future endeavors could suffer, or benefit, as well.

In order to effectively launch a change initiative, a delicate equilibrium between careful planning and implementation must be struck. While it is inadvisable to merely leap into action, too much thought can actually lead to immobility of sorts, thereby stalling the change completely. Think about this as akin to planning a car trip. A person can spend an inordinate amount of time mapping out a route, thinking about what to pack, preparing the automobile for the excursion, researching gas prices along the planned route, trying to predict issues or problems along the way and how to minimize these, booking accommodations at anticipated stopping points and coordinating with the other people who will be the traveling companions. In fact, a person can get stuck in a state of analysis paralysis and never get out of the planning mode. In contrast, if a person merely jumps in the car without any forethought and coordination with the other people who are also taking the journey, it is likely that something important will be forgotten or something along the journey will go wrong, yet this could have been avoided with proper preparation. This ultimately necessitates a return to the starting point and perhaps, if possible, restarting the journey again after more thought and planning have occurred. Often this restart is not possible, as the people involved become so put off and fed up by a failed journey that they do not wish to try again. It is important to remember that when you travel with others, the journey cannot begin until everyone is ready.

The key point is that eventually, the people who want to end up in a different location need to get into the car and head off on the trip. Remaining in the planning stage and never actually getting in the vehicle is not effective. Think about it. Do you have a friend or coworker who always *talks a big game*, but never actually gets anything done? Similarly, getting in the car and taking off without any deliberation and thought can be equally dangerous. Therefore, an effective way to launch change is to review critical considerations that must be addressed when activating change. Another way to think about this is the importance of assessing an organization's readiness for change. Just as a needs assessment should be conducted at the task, person and organizational level before a decision is made to offer any form of training or development, so too should a readiness assessment take place before a change begins. This, in turn, illuminates how to effectively plan *and* take action, thereby striking the correct balance between preparation and implementation.

Assessing Readiness

When commencing a change initiative there are key factors that should be examined and acknowledged. Doing so evaluates how prepared an organization is for change and also prevents oversights, ultimately leading to more effective change for both current and future organizational efforts. While the following categories could be deemed to overlap, it is useful to assess readiness for change using the training needs assessment framework of the task, person, and organizational levels. Further, it should be noted that many of the readiness considerations can be addressed through proper use of the formula for managing change. While it may appear to be overly simplistic, the reality is that effective enactment of the formula ultimately serves to remove many issues that detract from successful commencement of a change. A deeper exploration of these considerations further illuminates this point.

Task Level

A basic consideration when launching change is the actual requirement for the amendment. In other words, is the change really needed or necessary? When commencing a change this question must have a ready and apparent answer. Aligned with increasing dissatisfaction with the status quo, this will enhance the willingness of others to begin thinking about and/or doing things differently.

Further, when a change is launched it is important to give consideration to the amount of time required to successfully enact the modification. The scope and complexity of a change (what is actually involved in the *task of change*) is often underestimated and therefore anticipated timelines are too short or unrealistic. A practical understanding of what a change actually involves and requires may lead to consideration of a phased approach. An incremental approach with smaller steps, and an allocation of more time, may be a more strategic and effective way to commence modifications. Again, with the utilization of planned steps, a comprehensive albeit slower approach can be presented when a change is begun, thereby ultimately supporting a successful outcome.

Person Level

It is imperative to assess how ready the people involved in the change are for this to begin. Consideration of people's openness and eagerness to commence thinking about or doing things differently is critical. This can be accomplished through an understanding of the shared and compelling need, trust, and fatigue.

Shared and Compelling Need

When a change is launched there must be a common and driving force that people can engage with and support.[2] Those requesting the change often forget this critical point. Those driving the change already comprehend why it is needed and support the modification, but often forget that this level of understanding and buy-in is not widespread. As such, this aligns with increasing the dissatisfaction with the status quo and increasing the vision, as highlighted within the formula for managing change. When a change is not begun with appropriate planning, people impacted by it will likely not have a combined understanding of why the change is required and what the desired outcome is, and as such are not ready to change. As previously noted, without these forces the desire and support for the change lessens. In comparison, a successful launch capitalizes on dissatisfaction and vision, and by increasing these it unites people to support, believe in, enact, and then maintain the change.

Trust

The initial way that change is introduced will have implications on how much people are able to trust the process, the leaders who are requesting the modification, and the proposed benefits of the outcome. Aligned with core resistance, if those impacted by and/or involved in the change do not trust the process and those requesting the amendments, poor outcomes will ensue.[3] As with shared and compelling need, those initiating and desiring a change already have developed trust and therefore often forget that this will likely not be widespread. As a result, the requirement to develop trust, both in the process and outcome, is often not given ample consideration. As previously noted, through an increase in dissatisfaction with the status quo and an increase in the vision, coupled with a strong plan (steps) and lowering of key resistance points, trust in the process and desired outcome can be enhanced. Plans and processes to ensure that this is accomplished at the very start of a change initiative are therefore critical.

Fatigue

When change is launched ample consideration to what people are able to cope with is often not given full consideration. As such, examination of current change initiatives, overall workload, stress levels, and capacity (both mental and physical) should occur. Before launching a change it is important to take the time to reflect on whether people who need to enact and maintain the change are actually capable of doing so.[4] At times people are burned out and cannot, and will not, cope with any further demands on their time, energy, and resources. In other words, points of resistance will be too high and any commencement of change will not succeed. In these circumstances, it is often best to rethink the timing of the change as people are not ready and/or able to embrace any types of modifications. At times, delaying the commencement of a change initiative is actually a more strategic, effective alternative.

Organizational Level

When a change commences, it is important to have a deep understanding of the organizational elements or factors that will impact how the requested change is perceived and received. This can be accomplished through an examination of the following: history and culture.

History

As previously noted, an organization operates within a historical context and people remember previous change initiatives. As such, if an organization has a precedent of failed change initiatives, there may be resistance to trying something new (yet) again and a sense of dread that this is merely another request for change in a long string of ongoing, ill-thought-out demands.[5] In other words, people get sick and tired of ongoing change mandates. With a deeper understanding of what has gone on before (i.e., an organization's history and experiences with change initiatives), the launch of a change can be refocused and presented in a manner that shows it as different from what was previously encountered, which can eliminate, or at least minimize, how tired people are with responding to ongoing, similar requests for change. This is best accomplished by increasing the vision and by clearly demonstrating, right from the very start, how this desired outcome is not simply more of the same or a repeat of something that has already unsuccessfully been attempted.

It should also be noted that an understanding of previous change initiatives also serves to highlight what has gone well.[6] Using an appreciative inquiry approach, a launch of change can highlight and build upon what is currently working well in addition to success that has been experienced with previous change initiatives. Appreciative inquiry highlights that organizations are socially constructed entities and through a lens of optimism, positive consequences, and experiences can be leveraged and enhanced to bring about even better results.[7] As such, change can be launched by building upon, and reminding people about, previous experiences with successful change initiatives and outcomes. Appreciative inquiry encourages people to dream big and spring board off of what works well through deliberate actions, thereby highlighting how change should be commenced with a strong and increased vision as well as planned steps to reach this desired goal.

Culture

When commencing any change initiative it is critical to have an understanding of the context in which the amendment is occurring. As such, an organization's culture, and the expected behavior and interactions that have evolved from it, can have severe implications on how, and even if, a change begins.[8] Cultural factors can derail even the most minor changes, even tangential changes, as established patterns and rules are so established and entrenched that people do not want to entertain or consider any amendments. Therefore, it is critical to consider cultural elements and the potential effects that these will have on the launch of a change.

An organization's culture is descriptive and not evaluative. As such, value-laden statements or desirability do not play into this consideration. Instead, it is critical to recognize typical expectations that underlie how an organization operates, as these elements can and should be taken into consideration when launching change. The following are examples of questions that people typically consider with regard to their work and the responses are indicators of the culture within a company:

- What is the appropriate amount of personal disclosure?
- What is quality? How good is good enough?
- How much credit can I take for my work?
- What can I ask of my boss?
- Can I informally speak to my boss or should I book an appointment?
- What is the right amount of chit chat versus work?
- How should I dress?
- How much freedom do I have to decorate and personalize my work space?
- What is my work space like (i.e., size, location, furnishing) compared to what other people are given?
- How should I talk about outsiders/customers and other departments?
- How accurate does my work need to be?
- How punctual do I need to be?
- How much risk can I take in getting my work done?

Figure 6.1 highlights an example of some elements within a typical spectrum or range of standards within an organization, thereby further providing cues to the type of culture that people operate within.

The key point is that expected standards become so entrenched that if any change is deemed to be interfering with, or amending these norms, then it will be difficult for this change to even begin. Therefore, through a deeper and full understanding of an organization's culture, key points of

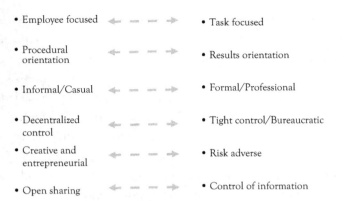

Figure 6.1 Organizational culture spectrum

opposition can be identified, anticipated, and responded to. In summary, organizational culture will highlight critical resistance points that can and should be acknowledged and lowered (as discussed in Chapter 5), or it is likely that a change initiative will not even get off the ground.

Beyond the Formula

While elements within the formula for managing change can be strategically used to focus on critical considerations when launching change, another deliberate and tactical approach is addressed through utilizing and attending to polarities. This purposeful methodology for launching change will now be reviewed.

Polarities

When launching change, there is a propensity to emphasize the positive possibilities that can be derived from the desired modification. While it makes intuitive sense to stress the anticipated constructive outcomes, this often results in what can be termed as *cheerleading* or *hype*. As such, what is meant to get people excited about a change in fact is interpreted as those requesting the change as having an unrealistic understanding of a situation, which in turn only serves to turn people off of a change as it is introduced. Or, an announcement of change is often received with resigned compliance. In such cases people will nod, agree, and appear to accept the change as it is launched, only to later ignore or avoid it. In order to avoid cheerleading and hype, or face a situation where people only pretend to accept the requested modification, utilizing and addressing polarities provides a balanced approach to launching change which, in turn, leads to increased acceptance, implementation, and maintenance of the requested adjustment. As the name implies, this approach addresses and accounts for anticipated polar opposites during times of change and thereby deals with the commencement of change in a way that acknowledges these differing, or contrary issues that should be acknowledged and addressed.

Utilizing and addressing polarities focuses on the following areas when launching change: why the change is needed, where the change is headed, and anticipated benefits, concerns with the change and anticipated support and what is not changing.[9] Each of these will now be examined in greater detail.

Why the Change Is Needed

Addressing polarities when launching change states that the first thing that must be conveyed is a clear message around why the change is required. In other words, the initial step is to ensure an understanding of what is driving the change and why the current circumstances will no longer suffice. It is interesting to note that this is in complete alignment with the concept of increasing dissatisfaction with the status quo, as addressed in the formula for managing change.

Where the Change Is Headed and Anticipated Benefits

The next part in introducing change is to clearly convey the direction of the change and the resulting benefits that will ensue. This aligns with increasing the vision, as per the formula for managing change, and also addresses the "what's in it for me?" question, thereby increasing dissatisfaction with the current situation by illuminating how much better/more effective/more enjoyable things could actually be if the requested change is implemented and sustained. Again, it is important to remember that the anticipated benefits must be those that people would value and appreciate and not merely a focus on positive corporate outcomes.

Concerns with the Change and Anticipated Support

Acknowledging polarities then requires that time be spent addressing why people may be unhappy or fearful about the change and the ways in which the organization is planning to respond to these concerns. It may seem rather counterintuitive to talk about problems or things that could go wrong and this is not likely something most people have encountered when a change is being introduced. However, doing so lets people know that those requesting the change have actually taken the time to think about and consider how this is impacting people and also want to implement ways to support people through the process. For example, it could be stated that there is anticipation that people may fear loss of job skills and, as such, training and development opportunities will be provided. Or, it is expected that people worry that they will lose access to key information and updates and therefore a communication plan has been developed and will be shared.

It is important to acknowledge that not all concerns have been, nor could be, thought of in advance and addressed. As such, this is also the chance to invite people to share their concerns and ideas for how to address them throughout the change process. When this is done during the launch of a change, and processes are actually put in place to ensure that this can be accomplished, it sets an inclusive and caring approach to the entire change management approach. Further, transparent and overt acknowledgment of concerns and anticipated responses to these issues helps to minimize and lower resistance points.

What Is Not Changing

Yet again, another counterintuitive measure is used through polarities, as the final step to launching change addresses the requirement to be transparent about what is *not* changing. Most people have not likely experienced introduction of changes where time is spent addressing what is valued and therefore will not be altered. However, by sharing what will not be modified, a sense of security and foundation is maintained. Further, people are less likely to feel overwhelmed as they realize that not all that is familiar will be lost. As such, through careful and purposeful sharing of what remains constant, a launch of change can serve to reassure people and ultimately lower their resistance.

Focus of Polarities

Given the four areas of focus when utilizing polarities, it is important to understand how much attention each of the areas should be given. For example, if a 10-minute speech was given to launch a change then the following time should be allocated:

- Why the Change Is Needed: 3 minutes
- Where the Change Is Headed and Anticipated Benefits: 2 minutes
- Concerns with the Change and Anticipated Support: 4 minutes
- What Is Not Changing: 1 minute

As depicted in Figure 6.2, the various elements should be stressed or attended to in an orderly and sequential manner, with a specific amount of time/focus allocated to each topic in order to effectively launch change.

Further, the subject matter and proportionate timing allocated to each step in the process should follow these guidelines for any and all types of initiatives (i.e., speeches, written announcements, meetings, press releases) in order to most effectively utilize polarities to launch change and fully experience the resulting benefits.

Benefits of Utilizing Polarities

As previously noted, addressing polarities provides a balanced and effective approach for launching change.[10] When implemented properly, the following benefits can be experienced:

- Preventing of cheerleading regarding the change.
- Presenting a balanced and credible approach to change.
- Fostering of a broader discussion about the change.

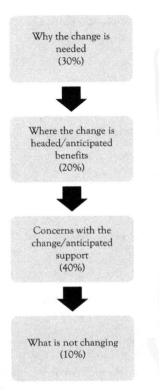

Figure 6.2 Utilizing and addressing polarities

- Encouraging a more complete analysis of the change situation.
- Enhancing understanding of the unsuitability of the current situation.
- Building buy-in for the change and trust in those requesting it.
- Conveying of a meaningful rationale and vision for change.
- Demonstrating empathy to those enacting and being impacted by the change.
- Addressing and lowering primary types of resistance: personal, intellectual, and core.
- Determining if the change is necessary and/or should be done in a more phased approach.

While not necessarily an intuitive or natural approach to launching change, addressing and working with polarities results in numerous advantages and addresses key issues that may be overlooked. It is therefore advisable for this process to be followed when commencing change.

Summary

Commencing a change initiative requires careful thought and planning, but it is important that people do not get mired down in merely thinking about the process and that the change is eventually put into action. Through a review and careful consideration of critical factors that influence and impact readiness for change, at the task, person, and organizational level, strategic use of the formula for managing change can be utilized to ensure successful commencement of a change initiative. Further, a polarized approach provides guidelines for how a change should be launched through the use of key messages and differing emphasis on these points.

While it is critical to effectively launch a change, it is then important to maintain momentum and ongoing action so that the desired modification does not merely fizzle out. This is the focus of Chapter 7.

End of Chapter Questions

- Think of a situation (personal or professional) when a change never got off the ground. Why do you think this occurred?
- Think of a situation (personal or professional) when a change began too quickly. Why do you think this occurred?
- Review the critical considerations to assess readiness for change. Which one of these factors was a key reason that the change you thought about was launched too quickly? As such, what could have been done differently to better ensure a successful start for the change?
- Based on your experiences, what are some other critical considerations when assessing readiness for change?
- Think of a change (personal or professional) that you will be commencing. How could you use polarities (draft a speech or plan) to launch this initiative?
- In addition to the benefits listed, what other positive outcomes could you foresee from using polarities to launch change?

CHAPTER 7

Maintaining Change Momentum

Belief in oneself is incredibly infectious. It generates momentum, the collective force of which far outweighs any kernel of self-doubt that may creep in.

—Aimee Mullins

A change initiative can begin with great enthusiasm and support, but unless maintained, any and all categories of change have the risk of never getting fully implemented or used. Even a tremendous launch to a change initiative does not guarantee ongoing, successful enactment of the amendment. Therefore, it is critical to ensure that once a change begins or is introduced, that it is actually implemented and enacted. This can best be accomplished with attention to the following: sponsorship, change agents, and ongoing utilization of the formula for managing change.

Sponsorship

Without backing from a member of an organization's senior leadership or executive team, a change initiative will eventually lose momentum.[1] When a leader, or person in a position of uppermost authority, is seen to be supportive of a change it provides legitimacy to the initiative. Simply put, if a change does not matter to someone in charge of, or within the top ranks of, an organization, it will not ultimately matter to others. An amendment may begin with great interest, but eventually people will discontinue support if there is not at least one member in the top management/leadership group continuously advocating for the amendment.

This leader, or person in a position of authority, who acts in this capacity is known as a sponsor of change. It is inevitable that new or different organizational initiatives and projects will occur and the sponsor makes sure that resources such as people, time, money, and equipment continue to be devoted to the change. This ensures that the organization displays commitment to the long haul and that new ideas and initiatives do not simply replace, or override, progress made to date and ongoing interest in a current change initiative. As well, a sponsor ensures that the change continues to be discussed and reviewed by the senior leadership team so that regular updates are provided to ensure ongoing awareness and knowledge of the change. Additionally, a sponsor should be vigilant about any resistance that may be occurring within the leadership group, as this will ultimately filter down and throughout an organization. It is incumbent upon the sponsor to address and minimize opposition to the change that is occurring within the leadership group. The tools and techniques reviewed in Chapter 5 can be utilized toward these efforts.

Further, the sponsor maintains change momentum by reminding an organization's leadership team why the change is needed, what the end state will be and how progress is being made toward this goal. Simply put, the sponsor utilizes elements within the formula for managing change to maintain support and interest in the change among those responsible for leading an organization. Without ongoing support from and within the group heading up an organization, disinterest in the change will occur at all levels throughout a company, resulting in the change initiative waning and ultimately being forgotten and dismissed.

As well, the sponsor should be willing to receive, and respond to, questions or concerns from other stakeholders impacted by the change. At key points in the change process the sponsor will have responsibility for delivering messages that align with, or bring to life, elements within the formula for managing change. This will be discussed further in Chapter 8. In summary, without a sponsor, no matter how vital, interesting, or enticing a change initiative is, it will ultimately lose traction and will not be effectively implemented.

While backing for a change initiative through a sponsor within the senior leadership group is critical, so too is maintaining ongoing support from all other people impacted by the change. Change agents play a critical role in ensuring that this occurs.

Change Agents

Support for, and belief in, a change initiative must be present *within the ranks*, so to speak. This means that among those people impacted by the change and those who must implement and maintain the change, there should be people who act as catalysts by reinforcing the promotion of the amendment.[2] Change agents help keep a change initiative thriving and bring a specific energy and focus through their actions. The importance of change agents is best illuminated through an understanding of their role and their characteristics.

The Role of Change Agents

Change agents are champions for the desired change. They are often viewed as a hub or central force for change.[3] This is due to the fact that people in these roles are conduits of information to and from the leadership group, and specifically the sponsor, to and from the people impacted by the change. Change agents do not speak for the sponsor, but do ensure that the sponsor's message is heard. As such, people in these roles are able to convey the importance of the change, using elements within the formula for managing change, in a convincing and enticing manner that encourages and energizes other people. Further, change agents are able to sense through what they hear, do not hear, see and *do not see* happening when a change is going off track and/or where key points of resistance are occurring. As well, change agents should be known as the people who others can turn to and share their worries regarding the change. With this knowledge, change agents are able to inform the sponsor of problems that are happening, thereby providing the opportunity for concerns to be addressed and rectified. In addition to updating the sponsor, change agents should provide advice and counsel on how to address concerns and how best to capitalize on things that are going well in order to ensure that momentum is maintained.

In summary, change agents are like internal advisors and consultants who provide a line of communication to and from the sponsor, ensure that the sponsor and thereby the leadership group are well informed about what is not working within the change process, and offer advice and ideas on how to keep the change initiative on track.

Change agents naturally arise during times of change, as some people gravitate to this type of role. In addition to those who are drawn to this, it is also strategic for people to be selected for these roles. There is a danger that if one waits for change agents to spontaneously arise this may never occur. The bigger concern is that without overt selection, or at least conscious recognition and acknowledgment of those fulfilling the role of change agents, support cannot be provided and change agents will not be effectively used during the change process. Therefore, determining who is taking on the role of a change agent is critical and to just let it happen and not attend to people in this capacity will undermine the progress of change. In other words, if change agents are not chosen and/or those who are fulfilling this role of their own accord are not supported, they will not be given the appropriate access to the sponsor and the flow of information will be stifled. Further, when change agents are acknowledged in a transparent manner, again either through being selected for this role or through being recognized for naturally fulfilling this role, people will know that these individuals are a resource to turn to for support and guidance during times of change. Finally, change agents must be recognized and supported, by both the sponsor and HR professionals, or they will burn out. Those giving support and encouragement to others during times of change need their own care and backing. Through open recognition of those acting as change agents, again either through selection and/or through self-selection, the role of change agents can be more effectively fulfilled during times of change. This will be further discussed in the next chapter regarding communication strategies during times of change. The key issue is that HR professionals need to be aware of who the change agents are, either through what is evolving during the change process or through overt selection of these individuals. Knowing the characteristics of effective change agents assists in this regard.

Characteristics of an Effective Change Agent

Given the significant and influential role that change agents hold, not every person is suited or appropriate to take on this function during times of change. The most obvious, but often overlooked factor is that change agents must be people who are supportive of the change. Only those who genuinely believe in and back the amendment can convince others to do so. Change agents must have a positive energy surrounding them and be very open about their desire for the change to move forward.

Change agents should be from the *rank and file* of an organization. In other words, these are people whom others can relate to, as they share common experiences, concerns, and understanding of what is occurring in a company. A change agent is best able to convince others that change is positive and should move forward if there is a shared appreciation of what the change is really asking for and the implications of the amendment. People are more apt to listen to and be convinced by those whom they share a connection with. If a person is seen as too far removed either due to formal positioning in an organization or due to lack of understanding of what the work involves and requires, then others will not be readily open to listen to and be influenced by this individual.

To that end, change agents must be people who others trust and respect.[4] As such, change agents are typically people who have been with an organization for a sufficient amount of time to become well known, well liked, and credible. The role of change agent is best suited to those who others feel comfortable opening up to, listening to, and who are seen as capable of fully understanding the implications of the change. A change agent is a charismatic influencer whom people are drawn to and admire. Not only must the change agent be respected and trusted by people within the organization, but the sponsor must also have the same sentiments as well. In order for a sponsor to listen to, accept advice, and act on information shared, the change agent must be seen as someone who is competent and reliable.

As well, given the role of conveying information to and from the sponsor, a change agent must be an effective communicator. In order to properly hear others and ensure that the ideas and concerns are shared, a change agent needs to be a good listener and then be able to convey concepts to others, both through written and spoken mechanisms. Further, change agents must be able to convey empathy for others, as this provides a feeling that one has actually been heard and understood. As previously noted, a change agent is a conduit of information and therefore must be capable of ensuring that exchanges occur throughout the change process, thereby further driving the amendment forward.

While attending to and supporting the change sponsor and change agents is critical, HR professionals must also ensure that the formula for managing change is continuously employed, as this too will provide ongoing momentum for the sought-after change.

Ongoing Utilization of the Formula for Managing Change

Even when people react to the start of a change in a positive manner, and the first steps show that the change is moving forward, this progress can quickly dissipate if there are strong points or resistance. Often, it is only when a change begins to be implemented that people's concerns are felt and brought to light. Key methods to lower resistance were examined in Chapter 5 and use of these tools and techniques will help a change advance. It is critical that these issues are revisited and re-examined throughout the change process. Effective change management requires ongoing consideration of, and reaction to, resistance, and it is imperative that this not be a one-time occurrence that is believed to have been adequately dealt with and therefore never given further attention and action. Just as the enactment of change evolves, so too do the potential feelings and reactions due to resistance. Continued examination of resistance means that HR professionals must constantly be in touch with, and aware of, how people are, or are not, effectively implementing and/or continuing to enact the change. This necessitates ongoing opportunities for people to communicate concerns regarding the change as well as ongoing methods for HR professionals to assess and respond to resistance. Tools and techniques to ensure that this occurs will be addressed in Chapter 8.

Just as resistance is not something that can be examined and dealt with at one singular point in the change process, ongoing attention must be given to dissatisfaction with the status quo, the vision, and the steps toward change. At key points during the enactment of change, people must be reminded why the change was necessary, what the desired future state is, and that progress is being made and celebrated. When this occurs, the ongoing implementation of change is enhanced. As previously noted, tools and techniques to ensure that this transpires will be addressed in Chapter 8.

Summary

A successful start to a change initiative does not guarantee successful implementation and enactment of the desired amendment. Impetus for change is best continued when a member of an organization's top leadership team takes on a sponsorship role for the initiative and therefore has a vested interest and involvement in the process. Further, key people throughout the organization who are impacted by the amendment and strongly believe in and support it can keep the process moving forward by acting as change agents. These people fulfill a critical role by acting as liaisons between the sponsor and those impacted by the change and by helping to ensure ongoing awareness and communication about the change, which in turn drives things forward. Charismatic and trustworthy people who themselves believe in and support the change can, in turn, help others buy into the change and therefore help to move the initiative forward. In addition to the critical roles of sponsor and change agents, ongoing attention to, and use of, elements within the formula for managing change also serve to help the change initiative progress.

Strategic communication plays a key part of maintaining momentum for change, whether through a sponsor, change agents, and/or use of the change formula. Skillful and tactical communication is also required when launching change, so it is a key requirement at all points throughout the change process and this is the focus of the next chapter.

End of Chapter Questions

- Who in your organization would be an effective sponsor of change? Why did you select this person? What could you do to support the person fulfilling this role?
- Who in your organization possesses the qualities of an effective change agent? What could you do to support the person fulfilling this role?
- What other qualities, in addition to the characteristics presented in this Chapter, should an effective change agent possess? Why did you select these characteristics?

- Do you think that it is more common for people to naturally take on the role of change agent or is it more common for people to be formally appointed to these roles? What are the pros and cons of each occurrence?
- Why might people refuse to take on the role of change agents when asked to do so? What could you do to convince them to take on this function?

CHAPTER 8

Communication

Wise people speak because they have something to say; Fools because they have to say something.

—Plato

A key component of change management is a strategic communication plan that supports and reinforces the desired amendment. This means that a carefully thought out and deliberate approach to delivering messages or information is required. When there is a lack of news, particularly during times of change, there is a tendency for people to fill the void and create their own understanding.[1] As such, without a purposeful approach for communicating, false messages and rumours will often ensue and detract from, or completely derail, a change initiative.

As well, communication during times of change is critical for enacting the various components within the formula for managing change. Increasing dissatisfaction with the status quo, increasing the vision, implementing and celebrating the planned steps, and decreasing resistance all rely on effective conveyance of information. As such, effective change management also involves the creation of a deliberate, tactical communication plan. In essence, strategic communication helps create buy-in, support, desire, and action for change. This, in turn, enhances the way change is launched, advanced, and ultimately sustained. The aforementioned points address *why* communication is needed during times of change and deeper exploration of this topic can be done through consideration of the following other elements within the journalism model: who, what, when, and how/where.[2]

Who

At its core, an effective communication strategy focuses on people. This can best be thought of as addressing who should be receiving the communication and who should do the communicating.

Who Should Receive Communication

The first component of effective communication is customizing and crafting messages to the intended audience(s). This necessitates a clear understanding of who needs to receive and understand messages and is often an area that is not given adequate consideration during times of change. This is due to the fact that time is not taken to thoroughly consider who the stakeholders, or people impacted by, or interested in, a change are. Therefore, it is critical to take a step back, per se, and think deeply about the implications of a change. This process, which is supported by an understanding of the driver(s) and type(s) of change, helps to illuminate whom within an organization the change will have an effect on. At first blush it appears that an amendment will only influence people within an organization, but others, external to the organization are often involved as well. As such, a stakeholder analysis, or stakeholder map, should be developed to identify all those who need to know about and/or understand a change. This tool helps to ensure that communication plans are developed to address *all* people impacted by a change initiative.

Who Should Communicate

The source of information is as critical as the messaging itself, particularly during times of change.[3] Therefore, communication should come from those who are respected, trusted, and seen as credible sources of information. When this does not occur, messages tend to be ignored or viewed as inaccurate and the intended impact is not achieved. As such, communiqués tend to be most effective when presented by people who are thought to truly understand how a person is impacted by a change. In such circumstances these are typically employees' immediate supervisors and/or change agents.[4] This is a critical point, as ongoing communication throughout the change process is best delivered to employees from those whom they report to and/or those who are trusted and respected catalysts for change.

Ongoing legitimacy and attention to a change initiative is also provided through communication from the sponsor and/or key leaders of an organization. At key junctures in the change process, messaging from those in senior positions plays a critical role in ensuring that the initiative is taken seriously and implemented. For example, the launch of a change should be communicated using polarities from the top leader of an organization. This messaging can then be reinforced by direct supervisors and change agents. While communication from supervisors and change agents has the most influence and impact, other leaders within an organization also have a role to play. At certain points in the change process key messages, from those leading an organization serve to keep people informed about, interested in, and supportive of a desired change.

While ongoing communication to employees is required, it is important to remember that all stakeholders, including those external to an organization, must continue to be informed. Therefore, based on the stakeholder map that was developed at the commencement of a change, the correct people should be identified to deliver messages to those external to an organization, who will be impacted by change. Depending on the relationships already established between those internal and external to an organization, these may be change agents, key leaders, or the change sponsor. The key point is that the person delivering messages to external stakeholders should be someone they respect, trust, and have a previously established communication pattern and rapport with.

At points throughout a change initiative, updates can be provided by HR professionals or the team tasked with implementing the change. However, it must be noted that this person or group is not the key resource for delivering messages throughout the change. Those impacted by change will *not* be most motivated or engaged by communiqués from change experts. Further, HR professionals are not communication specialists and therefore any and all forms of communication should ideally be written and vetted by people who have specific training and expertise in this area. As such, when an organization has a communications or media relations department, these people should be involved in creating all messaging, both for internal and external sharing.

An important take away from the previously noted considerations is that there is no magic bullet or one easy solution for who should communicate. The key issue is that careful thought and planning should be given as to who can most effectively (given the change, the organizational context, the stage in the change process, and the success and progress of the change to date) reach and influence the targeted stakeholder(s). As well, consideration must be given not only to the official role that the person communicating holds (and therefore their level of credibility and respect from others), but to their communication abilities and competencies as well. Some people are not suited for communicating to and with others and it is incumbent upon HR professionals to have a working knowledge of who in an organization should, and should not, be asked to fulfill this role during the change management process. At times, choice will not be given (i.e., it could destroy your career to tell the president of the company that he or she is not an effective communicator and therefore should not announce the launch of a change), but often during the change management process an HR professional will, and should, have a role to play in identifying who should be delivering key messages and will also be responsible for supporting people in these capacities. As such, knowing how to identify and choose key people in this regard is critical. And while, as previously addressed, HR professionals are not communication specialists, they also have a key role to play in determining what to communicate during times of change.

What

Through effective utilization of elements within the formula for managing change, HR professionals are able to ensure that important messages are conveyed at key junctures in the change process. As well, careful use of polarities can enhance the launch of change in addition to messages that specifically serve to increase dissatisfaction with the status quo, increase the vision, and address and celebrate the steps toward change and lowering of resistance. Therefore, the messages that need to be shared, the what, will vary based on which element within the formula for managing change is being addressed, the stage of the change process (e.g., is it launching or is it momentum being sustained?) and the success and progress of the change to date (e.g., have specific issues or points of resistance been noted and therefore must be addressed?). Simply put, the content of any communication must reflect an identified need within the change management process and be crafted to strategically respond to this requirement while reinforcing or addressing an element within the formula for managing change and/or polarities. HR professionals are best positioned to ensure that this occurs.

When considering what communiqués should contain, it is also critical to ensure that the messaging given to any and all stakeholders is consistent.[5] While the exact content can and should be customized based on the intended recipients, as the exact wording will be different to be best understood and valued by the different recipients, the overall information conveyed must be consistent across all impacted people.[6] Without a uniform message confusion will ensue, resulting in the stalling or even eventual prevention of the desired change. In addition to what is conveyed, timing of messages to all stakeholders is also an important consideration.

When

To ensure that key stakeholders receive similar messages, the timing of communication is also a critical consideration. While unexpected communication needs will arise due to unforeseen circumstances or resistance points that need to be quickly responded to, an overall plan for the timing of key messaging should be created and monitored. Ongoing communication is critical if change is to be implemented and sustained.

All communication should align with the timing of key points or milestones in a change management process and if/when the occurrences of these milestones shift, then so too should the communiqués. Further, HR professionals, when properly doing their role within the change process by maintaining awareness of how the change is, or is not, progressing, are in the best position to determine when communication needs to be delivered to support the change and/or minimize arising resistance. It is also important to maintain consistency of communication across and for all people impacted by the change.[7] When all stakeholders receive some form of communication at the same points in time, this aids in the realization of effective change.

It is also critical to build in plans to communicate even if full information is not known or obtainable. While it may seem counterintuitive to plan for messaging when no new or no information at all is available, without ongoing updates people will create facts and this is often the reason rumors spread, especially during times of change.[8] As such, it is important that a communications plan has ongoing, regular points/times to deliver messages to stakeholders. Especially during times of change, the familiar axiom of "tell them, tell them and then tell them again" applies. Stakeholders need to hear the same messages, in different ways and customized to best suit the target audience, on a continuing basis.

Further, ongoing messaging prevents people from speculating and creating false information, maintains momentum for and interest in change and addresses stakeholders' needs and/or advises them that further information is forthcoming.[9] This is a delicate balancing act, as silence is not golden, but at the same time stakeholders should not be overwhelmed or bombarded with continuous, low-value messages as they will then eventually ignore any and all communiqués. As such, the drafting of a plan of when to communicate around key milestones, coupled with additional communication at critical times to respond to unexpected issues, is an effective way to strike the correct equilibrium. Once again, HR professionals are best positioned to ensure that this occurs. Further effectiveness is also achieved through the choice of the communication medium or channel.

How/Where

How a message is conveyed can be equally as important as what is being conveyed and by whom. It is such a critical consideration that Marshal McLuhan noted that "the medium is the message."[10] If the right mechanism or medium is not used, then the message(s) may be lost and the effort to share information can be wasted. Further, the richness of communication is a key consideration.[11] Face to face is deemed to be the most intense and deep form of communication, as two-way exchanges are readily available and nonverbal forms of messaging can be used as well. Impersonal, or mass written communication is thought to be the least rich form of communication, but it is often warranted if a large number of people need to be reached at the same time. The decision about the way in which to communicate therefore requires thinking about how best to reach the intended audience while still appropriately conveying the intent and content of the message, while ensuring timely and consistent delivery of the message. This requires careful and deliberate preplanning, coordination, and thought regarding the organization's culture, available resources, and the reasons behind the communication.

Given the aforementioned considerations, typical forms of communication that are used during times of change are:

- Memos
- Surveys
- E-mail
- Company intranet
- Town hall meetings
- Team meetings
- Leadership visits/presentations to department meetings

As previously noted, there is no magic bullet or one key way to communicate during times of change. Instead, how to most effectively reach stakeholders while keeping the integrity and timeliness of the messages must be considered when selecting the communication mechanism or medium.

In addition to how the message is conveyed, the meta message, or messaging behind the messaging, must be considered.[12] This concept highlights that in addition to the actual medium used, the context within which communication occurs is critical. As such, consideration must also be given to the following:

- Environment (large, sparse room versus a warm and welcoming set up)
- Location (on site versus off site, distance to travel to location or access information)
- Room arrangements (lighting, spacing, temperature, seating)
- Timing of meeting and timeliness of presenter(s)

The context, or meta messaging, within which communication occurs conveys information about how much recipients are respected and valued. Meta messaging will also impact how much two-way communication is encouraged, and ultimately given, as well as how well the messages are received and acted upon. As the people experts during times of change, HR professionals should be best able to plan for, and then monitor, how meta messaging is either diminishing or enhancing communications.

While HR professionals are not experts regarding communication strategy, as key resources for the people involved in a change (the human element of change), they must ensure that communication is given appropriate consideration and is effectively implemented throughout the change management process. This critical role that HR professionals play therefore requires further exploration.

HR Professionals' Responsibilities Regarding Communication

As previously noted, HR professionals are not communication specialists or experts and therefore should not assume this role and associated responsibilities during times of change. What HR professionals can, and should do, is provide input into the communications plan and give guidance to those given responsibility for communication. A key part of this is the identification of all stakeholders within a change initiative and given their focus and expertise in human issues, HR professionals are best positioned to do this. Further, HR professionals must monitor communication needs as well as what is actually happening with communications (who, what, when, and how/where) to be able to gauge the effectiveness of these efforts. When desired results are not achieved, it is then incumbent on HR professionals to acknowledge this and provide suggestions and ideas for how communication plans need to be adjusted and altered. As experts in the human aspects of change management, HR professionals can provide ideas, in the creation and delivery of various communiqués, to ensure that elements within the formula for managing change and/or utilizing polarities are effectively being utilized at appropriate times and in appropriate ways. Further, HR professionals can guide and counsel those delivering various forms of communication to ensure that these people know what is expected of them, that their own concerns or questions are being addressed, and that there is consistency and timeliness for sharing of critical information. To this end, and as previously noted, HR professionals play a key role in working with sponsors and selecting change agents and/or recognizing those who have naturally fallen into these roles and in ensuring that these people receive assistance and have a resource to turn to when they require advice and guidance. Those who are helping to drive a change forward need their own resources and counsel, and HR professionals should act in this capacity.

Further to this, HR professionals play a critical role in ensuring the provision of opportunities for two-way communication throughout the change process. It is critical that all stakeholders have the ability to provide feedback, ask questions, voice concerns, and receive responses to these inquiries.[13] To this end, HR professionals must ensure that space is created for stakeholders to share, and receive responses to, uncomfortable or resistance points, during change. Possible methods for operationalizing this include: confidential phone lines for verbal messages to be left with written follow-up distributed to all stakeholders; preset ongoing open meetings for open dialogue with senior leaders, sponsors, and/or change agents; and confidential intranet sites for submission of written questions/ concerns followed up by online posting of responses. It is critical that not only are there avenues for stakeholders to express their concerns, but responses must also be shared and distributed across stakeholder groups. Doing so ensures that those who have expressed concerns receive feedback and answers and also conveys this information to other stakeholders, who likely have similar questions or concerns. As noted in Chapter 5, when resistance from stakeholders is acknowledged and addressed, it can actually produce a positive influence regarding change. Therefore, ensuring that there is room for difficulty to be acknowledged and addressed means that HR professionals often need to coach those fulfilling key communication and/or leadership roles. When HR professionals do not stay on top of these issues, through careful monitoring of stakeholder reactions, responses, or absence of responses when invited to provide input, throughout the entire change process, there is a tendency for problems to be ignored or avoided, resulting in a lack of communication and ultimately producing ineffectual change.

So, while HR professionals should not be in charge of crafting the specific messages, nor should they necessarily be the people to deliver critical information, there is still an important role to be enacted during the change management process. Figure 8.1 provides a template that HR professionals can utilize to ensure that their role regarding effective communication is properly carried out during times of change.

Stakeholder	Key message	How message aligns with /supports change management formula and/or polarities	Message consistent across/for all stakeholders?	Who delivers?	Support for person delivering message	When?	How?	Feedback/ monitoring mechanisms (Opportunities for two-way communi- cation)

Figure 8.1 Communication planning template

Through deep understanding of the human needs within times of change, with use of the formula for managing change and polarities and through careful monitoring of ongoing and evolving communication requirements, HR professionals can possibly provide updates at some points during a change (i.e., there are times during the process that communication should be received from the HR/change experts), but most importantly should monitor and provide input into the development and evolution of a communications plan while giving advice and support to those crafting and delivering key messages. These actions help to ensure the enactment of effective communications in support of the desired change. Therefore, while not experts within this area, HR professionals do have a critical role to play regarding communication during change management.

Summary

A strategic communication plan is an integral component of effective change management. Although HR professionals are not communications specialists, they do have a vital role to play in this process. As those most familiar with the human side and people requirements during times of change, HR professionals must identify key stakeholders and ensure that all those impacted by a change receive timely and consistent information. Further, HR professionals must monitor and stay abreast of all communications to ensure that messaging supports and enhances the change process, must ensure that the correct people deliver key messages in the proper format and manner, and are supported while doing so). As well, HR professionals must monitor stakeholder reactions to ensure proper adjustment of communications, including provision of opportunities for stakeholders to express and receive responses to questions and concerns, in response to peoples' evolving needs and points of resistance. An understanding of considerations regarding who, what, when, and how/where within communications practice enhances an HR professional's ability to fulfill these expectations.

Supporting and providing input into the development and delivery of effective communication throughout the change management process is only one of the key roles that HR professionals must enact. As such, further exploration of other critical functions for HR professionals during times of change is the focus of the next chapter.

End of Chapter Questions

- Think of a recent change that your organization experienced. Were all stakeholders properly identified? If not, why were some forgotten or omitted?
- What would you do if a senior manager/leader wanted to be the person to communicate a key message during change and you thought that he/she was not the best person to deliver this message?
- Think of a key message that you would want to deliver to a stakeholder during a change. How could you craft different messages, in different formats, so that you have delivered the same, critical information multiple times while not bombarding people with too much communication? How can you strike a balance between enough and too much communication?
- Given the culture in your organization, what is the best way (or best ways) to communicate during times of change? Why did you select this method (these methods)?
- Given the culture in your organization, what is the best way (or best ways) to ensure that stakeholders are able to communicate their concerns during times of change? Why did you select this method (these methods)? How would you ensure that responses are given to the concerns that are expressed?

CHAPTER 9

Bringing It All Together: The HR Professional's Role

Thinking about your role will automatically get you in the frame of mind to get your strategy and game plan right before you step onto the field.

—Harbhajan Singh

As explored throughout this text, change management is a multifaceted and complex competency that requires a skillful blend of scientific application and judgment. Further, as previously highlighted in Chapter 1, HR professionals are tasked with balancing the operational and emotional requirements of both employers and employees in order to enable efficient and effective attainment of corporate objectives. A key role within this responsibility is anticipating, responding to, guiding, and sustaining change.[1]

However, at the core of the matter and in reality, HR professionals are often given a great deal of responsibility in managing change, but little authority. It is ultimately people, at all levels throughout a company, but particularly senior managers or those in top leadership roles, who have the ability to actually drive change. I often hear HR colleagues' concerns that their advice is not being followed or that they are not being invited to be involved in implementing change and then yet, when amendments are not occurring as hoped and planned, they are called to fix problems, suggest course corrections, or explain why plans for change are amiss. While change is complex, the answer of how to avoid these problems and be a meaningful contributor to, and resource for, change initiatives is rather straightforward. HR professionals need to be known as experts and guides who share information, techniques, and tools, thereby ultimately helping others to embrace, utilize, and sustain different ways of acting and achieving results. So how does one do this? How does one become a trusted and sought-after resource pertaining to change management? HR professionals are best positioned to achieve success in their roles, in all aspects of their jobs but particularly pertaining to change management, through being aware and being vocal.

Being Aware

Possessing a keen and up-to-date understanding of what is impacting an organization, both internally and externally, is a critical component within an HR professional's role. Keeping abreast of forces for change enables HR professionals to better anticipate how to alter key organizational practices, procedures, and guidelines to ensure the ongoing success of a company. It is not always possible to anticipate required changes, so reactions to forces for change are therefore also important, but can only effectively occur through understanding and acknowledging these requirements. Environmental, market, and internal forces can be understood through ongoing monitoring of the business environment (locally and globally), reading news and social media posts (both internal and external offerings), staying informed about trends and important events, and actively networking with other professionals and contacts. To think that HR professionals only need to understand HR is both limiting and naïve. It is critical to be observant of the context that the company operates within, stay abreast of changes within this, and then support alignment of polices, guidelines, and practices through appropriate amendments. As such, it is best to think of HR professionals as business people who specialize in Human Resource Management. This can only be accomplished by remaining aware of the forces that are impacting the company and its stakeholders. This, in turn, assists HR professionals in knowing when and how to be vocal during change initiatives, as will be addressed later in this chapter.

A deeper understanding of the forces driving change also enables HR professionals to have a clear understanding of the category of change(s) being experienced. This, in turn, helps to develop a clear picture of the scope of the change, possible pitfalls, and the most strategic ways to aid in the promotion and sustainment of the desired amendment. In order to truly add value within the change management process and be a valued resource, HR professionals must be analysts and be willing to think deeply about what is actually occurring. In my experience, many HR professionals would not describe themselves as analytical, but this type of approach is required in order for the change management process to be successful. Time and effort taken to think deeply about change and study what is occurring will lead to better responses to, and engagement with, the people dealing with change.

In addition to remaining vigilant about the forces driving change and the category of change, it is equally critical for HR professionals to be observant about people's reactions to change. Doing so allows for a true understanding of what is occurring not just at a superficial level, but at a deeper more meaningful level. One method to accomplish this is through surveys and providing opportunities for stakeholders to give feedback.[2] HR professionals must ensure that all key stakeholders are identified and given the opportunity to provide input or response. As previously addressed in the text, HR professionals are often best positioned to determine who will be impacted by change. Therefore, while not necessarily crafting or delivering messages, nor always being present during the actual opportunities for input, HR professionals can increase awareness for themselves and others during times of change by ensuring that all impacted people are involved, both through communication given to them and opportunities to provide feedback. Other ways to accomplish this are through providing stakeholders with opportunities for scheduled meetings with top leaders and/or the change sponsor and/or change agents. The key issue is that true awareness (for HR professionals and others impacted by the amendment) of what is occurring during times of change cannot occur without overt ways to encourage engagement and input from those impacted by it, and HR professionals must take on the role of ensuring that all stakeholders have opportunities to do so.

Further, HR professionals who are truly aware understand their organizations and people and can *sense* when things are on track or when things are not right. This understanding further enables HR professionals to assess an organization's readiness for change and how best to launch change. While it may seem strange for a professional text to be addressing intuition or the ability to *feel* what is occurring within a company, it is important to recognize that the practice of HR is both an art and science. To steer away from raising this point would be a disservice, both to the profession and those within it. Part of being aware means that HR professionals need to keep their fingers on the pulse of an organization, or in other words, be continuously aware of company culture, messages and communication that are being shared (often in the form of rumors or people filling in gaps of information), and peoples' behavior. Doing so allows for anticipation of and/or reaction to resistance points to change, as well as monitoring of ongoing support for the change at all levels across the organization and helps to gauge how well the change is, or is not, progressing. HR professionals must be on the lookout not only for what is being said and done, but also for what is not occurring or what is not being said. The absence of worries or concerns does not necessarily mean that a change is progressing, being implemented and being sustained. Often, when no concerns are present, this should signal that stakeholders are not actually engaging with or understanding the change. HR professionals should remain ever vigilant to the silence that can, in fact, be speaking volumes.

Further, being aware allows HR professionals to know which people in an organization are key influencers, which people are key communication sources, and who is respected by others, thereby assisting in the identification of change agents. It is only through true understanding of what is happening in an organization that HR professionals will know which people can, and should, be key resources and allies during times of change. This is critical, as the identification of change agents is a key role that HR professionals should play during times of change.

Awareness is achieved through an open door policy as people must know that they can approach you as a trusted and knowledgeable resource and by being visible to others. HR professionals who think that they can develop awareness solely from the confines of their offices to so as their own peril. Being aware involves participation in employee initiatives, walking around, talking to others, and being actively involved in the work that is happening in an organization. Being aware necessitates being seen and being involved. In essence, being aware is the only way in which HR professionals can develop a true understanding of the culture and key issues within their organizations.

The critical point is that in order to be aware of what is happening during times of change, HR professionals, through involvement and support of various initiatives in the organization, should have developed a reputation as a key resource long before a change begins. Being known for expertise and willingness to work with others to accomplish organizational goals, through previous contributions and accomplishments, will enable HR professionals to develop deep awareness of what is happening within an organization. Previous work and achievements will increase the likelihood that HR professionals will be asked to be involved in change activities and will also provide HR professionals with deep organizational awareness. In sum, HR professionals must view their ongoing role as one of developing deep organizational understanding, both through formalized and more informal measures, and will then be able to capitalize on this awareness during times of change.

While awareness is critical, this understanding will be ineffective if HR professionals are not able to vocalize or share their change management expertise. As such, a key element with HR professionals' roles is knowing when and how to convey knowledge and ideas.

Being Vocal

In order to be a trusted and utilized resource during times of change, HR professionals must be known for their actions and abilities to get things done. This can only be accomplished through active involvement or by being vocal about what needs to happen for change to be successful. As a starting point, HR professionals who, through their keen awareness know and understand the changes impacting their organizations, should request to be part of the change management process if they are not asked to do so. As previously noted, HR professionals are often frustrated by not being engaged in change, but instead should view this in a more assertive or overt manner.[3] When change is occurring, or better yet before a change commences, HR professionals must ask to be involved. In lieu of waiting for an invitation, strategic HR professionals are willing to speak to key decision makers and convey the benefits of their contributions to, and participation in, this work.

Using the tools and resources addressed throughout this text enables HR professionals to vocalize, or share, their change management expertise. Using knowledge of forces for change and categories of change, and addressing key elements within the formula for change enables HR professionals to convey crucial ideas and information to critical stakeholders. Further, understanding of resistance to change, launching change, and maintaining momentum enables HR professionals to articulate critical elements and required processes and tasks within change management. As well, and as detailed in Chapter 8, HR professionals need to contribute to communications planning and implementation. This text has provided numerous tools and resources to enact and bring about meaningful and lasting organizational change, but this knowledge must be shared with others through tactful and well-thought-out dialogue with stakeholders. As such, HR professionals should view their change management role as being a guide or facilitator. This necessitates using change tools and techniques, asking for face time with leaders and change sponsors at critical points in the change process, actively engaging with while supporting change agents and customizing messages so that all stakeholders understand and can relate to what is being shared. The HR professional's role is therefore to take change management knowledge and translate it into language and messages that stakeholders can understand and embrace. This is not an easy task, as HR professionals will need to be brave enough to use their awareness and insights to approach and engage key stakeholders through tactful and meaningful discourse.

While not always comfortable, HR professionals need to have the courage to speak up and be willing to work with stakeholders, even if this means addressing unpleasant topics or situations. HR professionals should not shy away from exchanges that will identify and address resistance points, illuminate when change is not progressing, identify when launching change has not been well thought out, and when momentum for the change is not being correctly addressed. As detailed in Chapter 5, there are numerous tools and techniques for lowering resistance during times of change and HR professionals who identify key resistance points through their deep organizational awareness need to actively share these ideas with those who have the ability and authority to create the support systems and resources that can minimize resistance.

HR professionals must achieve a delicate balance of managing, yet facilitating and guiding others through the change process. At times this role will demand a more assertive approach, while still recognizing and attending to the power dynamics and formal organizational structure. At other times, the role demands a more gentle approach, involves listening, and displaying understanding and support. As such, championing the change management process requires great tact, diplomacy, and well-thought-out approaches for how to convey important information and concepts, at key points in time, in a manner that is consistent and yet targeted to/customized for various stakeholders. Through this approach, HR professionals are able to build change capacity in others, thereby providing strategic value within their change management roles.[4]

The ability to be aware and use this knowledge to vocalize, and therefore enact change management principles, is further enhanced when HR professionals are cognizant of their own beliefs, values, and responses to change. As such, self-understanding is also critical for an HR professional to be a valuable resource within change management.

Knowing Yourself

In order to be able to balance guiding and leading others through change, HR professionals should be aware of their own reactions to change. It is only through being mindful of one's own patterns of behavior and past experiences with change that assistance to others dealing with amendments can be given in a meaningful way. As such, part of an HR professional's role is self-reflection and self-understanding. It is therefore important that HR professionals take the time to think about their own potential roadblocks and resistance points to change. While unintentional if a person has negative feelings and responses to change, even if subconsciously, these will, in turn, detract from others embracing and bringing about new ways of acting. Through careful reflection and deeper understanding of oneself, potential self-imposed barriers to change can be lessened, thereby allowing for a more genuine and impactful way to help others with and through modifications.

As well, self-understanding enables HR professionals to better identify their strengths and where they can best lend change management expertise. It is important to have a clear picture of one's skills and competencies and where one needs further development. Knowledge of capabilities and potential points of weakness allows for ongoing self-development and personal growth. In addition to self-reflection, this understanding can also be achieved by asking others (family, close friends, and trusted colleagues) what they have observed regarding your reactions and responses during times of change. This self-exploration is not an easy task, as it requires vulnerability and a true desire for self-improvement.[5] However, time taken for heightened self- awareness, to look deeply and honestly at oneself, helps to enhance abilities to display and sustain your own effective change management behavior. This, in turn, allows HR professionals to act as role models and be of service to others during times of change.

Summary

HR professionals have a critical but not easy role to play regarding change management. In this capacity, a delicate balance of leading and guiding others is required. In order to add strategic value during times of change, HR professionals must remain ever aware of external forces, internal organizational factors, and stakeholder responses that are promoting or detracting from change. As well, HR professionals are tasked with speaking up, sharing change management expertise, and addressing and facing difficult situations and exchanges in a tactful and strategic manner. Further, HR professionals need to be self-aware, thus utilizing their change management strengths to the fullest while developing areas of weakness or minimizing their own points of resistance pertaining to change.

The opportunity to influence and assist others to enact meaningful and lasting organizational change is a privilege. While the journey during change management is complex, and certainly not for the faint of heart, it holds promise and potential to bring HR professionals some of the most exhilarating and fulfilling moments within their careers. As such, at the very heart of the matter, the change management role calls upon HR professionals to use their expertise, embrace challenges, capitalize on opportunities, and dare to make a positive, lasting and meaningful difference in the lives of others.

End of Chapter Questions

- How can you most effectively remain aware of forces for change that will impact your organization?
- What are some ways, which are appropriate within your organization's culture, to solicit feedback from key stakeholders throughout the change process?
- What steps can you take to ensure that you are remaining vigilant about what is not being said or done during times of change? How can you utilize silence to benefit change initiatives?
- What can you do to ensure that you are actively involved in change management initiatives within your organization?
- Think about your experiences and reactions to change. (Personal or professional examples). Based on this, what potential barriers or limitations could you have regarding change management? How will you minimize these?
- Again, think about your experiences and reactions to change. (Personal or professional examples). What particular strengths are you able to provide in times of change? How will you capitalize on these?
- Ask someone you trust and who knows you well about how you respond to change. Were you surprised by their feedback? What can you learn from their comments and use to enhance your role within change management?
- What have been your top three learnings from this text? What immediate changes to your own role and your actions can you implement based on this new knowledge?

Notes

Chapter 1

1. Stewart et al. (2017).
2. Heathfield (2016a).
3. CPHR/CRHA (2017); Human Resources Professional Association (n.d.); Society for Human Resource Management (2016).
4. Stewart et al. (2017).
5. Stewart et al. (2017).
6. Stewart et al. (2017).
7. Armstrong (2006).
8. Cooper (n.d.).

Chapter 2

1. Brockbank (1999).
2. Anderson and Anderson (2010).
3. Ulrich and Brockbank (2005).
4. Ulrich and Brockbank (2005).
5. Stewart et al. (2017).
6. Inness et al. (2010).
7. McKay-Panos (2013).
8. Melville and Bowal (2015).
9. Ulrich and Brockbank (2005).
10. Gerwing (2016).
11. Ulrich and Brockbank (2005).
12. Feurer et al. (1994).
13. Anderson and Anderson (2010).

Chapter 3

1. Carr, Hard and Trahant (1996).
2. Carr, Hard and Trahant (1996).
3. Anderson and Anderson (2010).
4. Van de Ven and Poole (1995).

5. Anderson and Anderson (2010).
6. Integrating Change Management and Project Management (n.d.).
7. Larson and Gray (2011).
8. Franklin (2014).
9. Anderson and Anderson (2010).
10. Barratt-Puch, Bahn, and Gakere (2013).

Chapter 4

1. Kotter (2002).
2. Kotter (2002).
3. Koeppel (2013).
4. Beckhard (1969); Dannemikller and Jacobs (1992).
5. Brecher (2015).
6. Gioia and Kumar (1991).
7. The formula for managing change typically addresses increasing the first steps, or ensuring that there are concrete actions at the beginning of the change process. However, I encourage increasing and attending to all steps through a planned approach (i.e., not just with the first steps) to promote enactment of the desired change.
8. Maurer (1996).
9. Maurer (1996).

Chapter 5

1. Maurer (2011).
2. Marris (2014).
3. Smith and Segal (2016).
4. Davis and Nolen-Hoeksema (2001).
5. Raven (1992).
6. Raven (1993).
7. Raven (1993).
8. Raven (1993).
9. Gannett (2013).
10. Raven (1993).
11. Raven (1993).
12. Raven (1993).
13. Tay and Diener (2011).
14. Gagné and Deci (2005).
15. Waddell and Sohal (1998).

Chapter 6

1. Maurer (2014).
2. Moran and Brightman (2000).
3. Crooner (2010).
4. Maurer (2011).
5. Maurer (2013).
6. Maurer (2013).
7. Watkins, Mohr, and Kelly (2011).
8. Jones (2010).
9. Johnson (1996).
10. Johnson (1996).

Chapter 7

1. Straker (2016).
2. Bartkus (1997).
3. Bartkus (1997).
4. Hartley, Benington, and Binns (1997).

Chapter 8

1. Gaffney (2006).
2. Buttry (2011).
3. Guffey, Loewy, and Almonte (2016).
4. Wikoff (n.d.).
5. Guffey, Loewy, and Almonte (2016).
6. Guffey, Loewy, and Almonte (2016).
7. Wikoff (n.d.).
8. Gaffney (2006).
9. Gaffney (2006).
10. McLuhan (1959).
11. Guffey, Loewy, and Almonte (2016).
12. Guffey, Loewy, and Almonte (2016).
13. Gaffney (2006).

Chapter 9

1. Hanson (2013).
2. Hines (2013).

3. Heathfield (2016b).
4. Ulrich (1998).
5. Schawbal (2013).

References

Anderson, D., and L.A. Anderson. 2010. "Beyond Change Management." In *Beyond Change Management*, by eds. D. Anderson and L.A. Anderson, 288. San Francisco: Pfeiffer.

Armstrong, M. 2006. In *Strategic Human Resource Management*, by ed. M. Armstrong, 194. New York, NY: Kogan Page.

Barratt-Puch, L., S. Bahn, and E. Gakere. 2013. "Managers as Change Agents: Implications for Human Resource Managers Engaging with Culture Change." *Journal of Organizational Change Management* 26, no. 4, pp. 748–64.

Bartkus, B.R. 1997. "Employee Ownership as Catalyst of Organizational Change." *Journal of Organizational Change Management* 10, no. 4, pp. 331–44.

Beckhard, R. 1969. *Organization Development: Strategies and Models*. Boston: Addison-Wesley.

Brainy Quotes n.d. Brainy Quotes. www.brainyquote.com/ (accessed February 3, 2017).

Brecher, N.D. 2015. "Two-Faced Fear: The Motivator and the Saboteur." *Journal of Property Management* 80, no. 3, pp. 22–23.

Brockbank, W. 1999. "Human Resource Management." In *Human Resource Management*, by ed. W. Brockbank, 337–52. 38 Vols. Hoboken, NJ: John Wiley & Sons Inc.

Buttry, S. 2011. "The 5 W's (and How) are Even More Important to Business than to Journalism." April 27. https://stevebuttry.wordpress.com/2011/04/27/the-5-w%E2%80%99s-and-how-are-even-more-important-to-business-than-to-journalism/ (accessed February 13, 2017).

Carr, D.K., K.J. Hard, and W.J. Trahant. 1996. *Managing the Change Process: A Field Book for Change Agents, Consultants, Team Leaders and Reengineering Managers*. New York, NY: McGraw Hill.

CPHR/CRHA. 2017. CPHR Canada. https://cphr.ca/ (accessed May 1, 2017).

Cooper, M. n.d. "Examples of Employer and Employee Conflicts." http://smallbusiness.chron.com/examples-employer-employee-conflicts-13804.html (accessed December 7, 2016).

Crooner, E. 2010. "Trust and Fairness During Strategic Change Processes in Franchise Systems." *Journal of Business Ethics* 95, no. 2, pp. 191–209.

Dannemikller, K.D., and R.W. Jacobs. 1992. "Changing the Way Organizations Change: A Revolution of Common Sense." *The Journal of Applied Behavioral Sciences* 28, no. 4, pp. 480–98.

Davis, C.G., and S. Nolen-Hoeksema. 2001. "Loss and Meaning: How Do People Make Sense of Loss?" *American Behavioral Scientist* 44, no. 5, pp. 726–41.

Feurer, R., and K. Chaharbaghi. 1994. "Defining Competitiveness: A Holistic Approach." *Management Decision* 32, no. 2, pp. 49–58.

Franklin, M. 2014. "3 Lessons for Successful Transformational Change." *Industrial and Commericial Training* 46, no. 7, p. 364. http://library.mtroyal. ca:2048/login?url=http://library.mtroyal.ca:2056/docview/1660133820? accountid=134 (accessed February 1, 2017).

Gaffney, S. 2006. *Honesty Works: Real-World Solutions to Common Problems at Work and Home.* Arlington: JMG Publishing.

Gagné, M., and E.L. Deci. 2005. "Self-Determination Theory and Work Motivation." *Journal of Organizational Behavior* 26, no. 4, pp. 331–62.

Gannett, A.K. 2013. "At Work: Job, self-Esteem Tied Tightly Together." August 31. www.usatoday.com/story/money/columnist/kay/2013/08/31/at-work-self-esteem-depression/2736083/ (accessed December 11, 2016).

Gerwing, M. 2016. "Two Superstore Locations Now Offering Click and Collect Services." May 25. http://winnipeg.ctvnews.ca/two-superstore-locations-now-offering-click-collect-services-1.2916534 (accessed January 2, 2017).

Gioia, D.A., and C. Kumar. 1991. "Sensemaking and Sensegiving in Strategic Change Initiation." *Strategic Management Journal* 12, no. 6, pp. 433–48.

Guffey, M.E., D. Loewy, and R. Almonte. 2016. *Essentials of Business Communication.* 8th ed. Toronto: Nelson Education.

Hanson, S. 2013. "Change Management and Organizational Effectiveness for the HR Professional." October 14. www.cornellhrreview.org/change-management-and-organizational-effectiveness-for-the-hr-professional/ (accessed February 1, 2017).

Hartley, J., J. Benington, and P. Binns. 1997. "Researching the Roles of Internal Change Agents in the Management of Organizational Change." *British Journal of Management* 8, no. 1, pp. 61–73.

Heathfield, S. 2016a. "Should You Join the Society for HR Management?" August 29. www.thebalance.com/society-for-human-resource-management-shrm-1918261 (accessed December 1, 2016).

Heathfield, S. 2016b. "The New Roles of the Human Resources Professional." October 12. www.thebalance.com/the-new-roles-of-the-human-resources-professional-1918352 (accessed February 10, 2017).

Hines, K. 2013. "5 Great Survey Tools to Get Feedback About Your Business." July 15. www.iacquire.com/blog/5-great-survey-tools-to-get-feedback-about-your-business (accessed February 8, 2017).

Human Resources Professional Association. n.d. www.hrpa.ca/ (accessed December 3, 2016).

Inness, M., T. Nick, J. Barling, and C.B. Stride. 2010. "OHS Transformational Leadership and Employee Safety Performance." *Journal of Occupational Health Psychology* 15, no. 3, pp. 279–90.

Integrating Change Management and Project Management. n.d. https://www.prosci.com/change-management/thought-leadership-library/integrating-change-management-and-project-management (accessed January 8, 2017).

Johnson, B. 1996. *Polarity Management.* Amherst: HRD Press.

Jones, G.R. 2010. *Organizational Theory, Design, and Change.* Upper Saddle River: Pearson.

Koeppel, M. 2013. "Change Management—Formula for Change." April 18. http://lakeletag.com/blog/2013/4/18/change-management-formula-for-change (accessed January 3, 2017).

Kotter, J. 2002. *The Heart of Change: Real-Life Stories of How People Change Their Organizations.* Brighton: Harvard Business Press.

Larson, E.W., and C.F. Gray. 2011. *Project Management: The Managerial Process.* Columbus: McGraw Hill.

Marris, P. 2014. *Loss and Change* (Psychology Revivals). New York, NY: Routledge.

Maurer, R. 2014. "Learning from the Failed Launches of Others." *The Journal for Quality and Participation* 37, no. 1, p. 33.

Maurer, R. 2013. "How to Lead Change Effectively by Learning from Past Setbacks." *The Journal for Quality and Participation* 36, no. 1, p. 28.

Maurer, R. 2011. "Why Most Changes Fail." *The Journal of Quality and Participation* 34, no. 2, p. 17.

Maurer, R. 1996. *Beyond the Wall of Resistance.* San Francisco: Jossey-Bass.

McKay-Panos, L. 2013. "New Developments in the Area of Discrimination on the Basis of Family Status." July 1. www.lawnow.org/discrimination-on-family-status/ (accessed February 1, 2017).

McLuhan, M. 1959. "Myth and Mass Media." *Daedalus* (MIT Press) 88, no. 2, pp. 339–48. www.jstor.org/stable/20026500?origin=JSTOR-pdf &seq=1#page_scan_tab_contents (accessed December 12, 2016).

Melville, L., and P. Bowal. 2015. "Mandatory Retirement: Not So Fast." March 9. www.lawnow.org/mandatory-retirement-not-so-fast/ (accessed February 4, 2017).

Moran, J.W., and B.K. Brightman. 2000. "Leading Organizational Change." *Journal of Workplace Learning* 12, no. 2, pp. 66–74.

Raven, B.H. 1993. "The Bases of Power: Originas and Recent Developments." *Journal of Social Issues* 49, no. 4, pp. 227–51.

Raven, B.H. 1992. "A Power/Interaction Model of Interpersonal Influence: French and Raven Thirty Years Later." *Journal of Social Behavior & Personality* 7, no. 2, pp. 217–44.

Schawbal, D. 2013. "Brene Brown: How Vulnerability Can Make Our Lives Better." April 21. www.forbes.com/sites/danschawbel/2013/04/21/brene-brown-how-vulnerability-can-make-our-lives-better/#5801d2ac60ba (accessed February 10, 2017).

Smith, M., and J. Segal. 2016. "Coping with Grief and Loss." At Work: Job, Self-Esteem Tied Tightly Together. October (accessed January 1, 2017).

Society for Human Resource Management. 2016. https://login.shrm.org/ (accessed December 3, 2016).

Stewart, E., M. Belcourt, M. Peacock, G.W. Bohlander, and S.A. Snell. 2017. "Essentials of Managing Human Resources." Nelson.

Straker, D. 2016. "Sponsorship of Change." http://changingminds.org/disciplines/change_management/planning_change/sponsorship_change.htm (accessed December 11, 2016).

Tay, L., and E. Diener. 2011. "Needs and Subjective Well-Being Around the World." *Journal of Personality and Social Psychology* 101, no. 2, pp. 354–65. doi:10.1037/a0023779 (accessed January 25, 2017).

Ulrich, D. 1998. "A New Mandate for Human Resources." January-February. https://hbr.org/1998/01/a-new-mandate-for-human-resources (accessed February 10, 2017).

Ulrich, D., and W. Brockbank. 2005. "The HR Value Proposition." In *The HR Value Proposition*, by eds. D. Ulrich and W. Borckbank. Brighton: Harvard Business Press.

Van de Ven, A.H., and M.S. Poole. 1995. "Explaining Development and Change in Organizations." *Academy of Management Review* 20, no. 3, pp. 510–40.

Waddell, D., and A.S. Sohal. 1998. "Resistance: A Constructive Tool for Change Management." *Management Decision* 38, no. 8, pp. 543–48.

Watkins, J.M., B.J. Mohr, and R. Kelly. 2011. *Appreciative Inquiry: Change at the Speed of Imagination.* 2nd ed. Hoboken: Pfieffer.

Wikoff, D. n.d. "How to Communicate Effectively Within the Change Process." www.reliableplant.com/Meta/Tags/talent%20management (accessed December 12, 2016).

Index

Assessing readiness
  beyond the formula, 66
  organizational level, 63–66
  personal level, 62–63
  task level, 61–62

Change agents, 75–78
  characteristics of, 76–78
  role of, 75–76
Change management, 5–6. See
        also Tangential change;
        Transformational change;
        Transitional change
  attending to steps, 37–41
  communication, 81–91
  dissatisfaction with status quo and,
        32–35
  formula for, 31–44, 78
  increasing vision, 35–37
  launching, 59–71
  overview, 9
  resistance and, 41–43
Change momentum, 73–80
  change agents, 75–78
  sponsorship, 73–74
Change, categories of
  interplay among, 28
  overview, 19–20
  tangential, 20–22
  transformational, 25–28
  transitional, 22–25
Cheerleading, 66
Coercive power, 47
Communication/communicate, 54,
        81–91
  how/where, 86–88
  HR's responsibilities for, 88–90
  planning template, 90
  what to, 84–85
  when to, 85–86
  who to, 81–84

Compensation, 5
Competitors, 13–14

Dissatisfaction
  tangential change and, 34–35
  transformational change and, 35
  transitional change and, 35

Expert power, 48–49

Fatigue, 63

HR designations, 1
Human Resource (HR) professionals
  being aware, 94–97
  being vocal, 97–99
  change management and, 5–6
  competitors, 13–14
  customer demands, 14
  expectations, 1
  as heart of organization, 3–4
  industry trends, 11–12
  labor market conditions, 12–13
  legislative requirements, 11
  organization's strategic goals and,
        10–11
  organizational strategies, 15
  overview, 1–3
  responsibilities regarding
        communication, 88–90
  roles, 1–3, 93–100
  self-understanding, 99–100
  strategic change management and,
        19–30
  work for, 4–5
Hype, 66

Industry trends, 11–12
Informational power, 49–50
Interpersonal relationships, 53–54

Labor market conditions, 12–13
Launching change
    assessing readiness, 61–66
    overview, 59–61
    polarities and, 66–69
Learning and Development, 5
Legislative requirements, 11
Legitimate power, 49
Lowering resistance, 51–54
    alignment of HR processes, 53
    communication, 54
    role analysis and requirements,
        52–53
    training and development, 51–52

Management. *See* Change
        management; Performance
        management

Organizational culture spectrum,
        66
Organizational level of change,
        19–30, 63–66
Organizational strategies, 15
Orientation, 5

Performance Management, 5
Person level
    fatigue, 63
    shared and compelling need, 62
    trust, 62–63
Polarities, of change
    acknowledging, 68
    addressing, 66–69
    benefits of, 69–71
    focus of, 69
Power
    and loss, connection between,
        46–51
    coercive, 47
    expert, 48–49
    informational, 49–50
    legitimate, 49
    referent, 50–51
    reward, 47–48

Recruitment and Selection, 5
Referent power, 50–51

Resistance
    benefits of, 54–56
    key areas of, 42
    lowering, 51–54
    to change. *See* Resistance to change
Resistance to change, 41–57
    connection between power and
        loss, 46–51
    overview, 45
    sense of loss, 45–46
Reward power, 47–48
Role analysis and requirements, HR,
        52–53

Sense of loss, 45–46
Self-reflection, 99
Self-understanding, 99
Sponsorship, 73–74
Steps
    tangential change and, 39–40
    transformational change and,
        40–41
    transitional change and, 40

Tangential change, 20–22
    dissatisfaction and, 34–35
    steps and, 39–40
    vision and, 36
Task of change, 61–62
Training and development, 51–52
Transformational change, 25–28
    dissatisfaction and, 35
    steps and, 40–41
    vision and, 37
Transitional change, 22–25
    dissatisfaction and, 35
    steps and, 40
    vision and, 36–37
Trust, 62–63

Vision
    overview, 35–36
    tangential change and, 36
    transformational change and, 37
    transitional change and, 36–37

Work Design, 5
Work-life balance, 5

OTHER TITLES IN THE HUMAN RESOURCE MANAGEMENT AND ORGANIZATIONAL BEHAVIOR COLLECTION

- *The Illusion of Inclusion: Global Inclusion, Unconscious Bias, and the Bottom Line* by Helen Turnbull
- *On All Cylinders: The Entrepreneur's Handbook* by Ron Robinson
- *Employee LEAPS: Leveraging Engagement by Applying Positive Strategies* by Kevin E. Phillips
- *Making Human Resource Technology Decisions: A Strategic Perspective* by Janet H. Marler and Sandra L. Fisher
- *Feet to the Fire: How to Exemplify And Create The Accountability That Creates Great Companies* By Lorraine A. Moore
- *HR Analytics and Innovations in Workforce Planning* By Tony Miller
- *Deconstructing Management Maxims, Volume I: A Critical Examination of Conventional Business Wisdom* by Kevin Wayne
- *Deconstructing Management Maxims, Volume II: A Critical Examination of Conventional Business Wisdom* by Kevin Wayne
- *The Real Me: Find and Express Your Authentic Self* by Mark Eyre
- *Across the Spectrum: What Color Are You?* by Stephen Elkins-Jarrett

Announcing the Business Expert Press Digital Library

Concise e-books business students need for classroom and research

This book can also be purchased in an e-book collection by your library as

- a one-time purchase,
- that is owned forever,
- allows for simultaneous readers,
- has no restrictions on printing, and
- can be downloaded as PDFs from within the library community.

Our digital library collections are a great solution to beat the rising cost of textbooks. E-books can be loaded into their course management systems or onto students' e-book readers.
The **Business Expert Press** digital libraries are very affordable, with no obligation to buy in future years. For more information, please visit **www.businessexpertpress.com/librarians**. To set up a trial in the United States, please email **sales@businessexpertpress.com**.

CPSIA information can be obtained
at www.ICGtesting.com
Printed in the USA
BVHW09s1524260718
522683BV00006B/105/P